365 Words of
Well~Being
for *Mothers*

365 Words of *Well-Being* for *Mothers*

RACHEL SNYDER

Contemporary Books

Chicago   New York   San Francisco   Lisbon   London   Madrid   Mexico City
Milan   New Delhi   San Juan   Seoul   Singapore   Sydney   Toronto

Library of Congress Cataloging-in-Publication Data

Snyder, Rachel.
365 words of well-being for mothers / Rachel Snyder.
p.   cm.
ISBN 0-07-140943-2
1. Motherhood—Miscellanea.   2. Mothers—Psychology—
Miscellanea.   3. Mother and child—Miscellanea.   I. Title: Three
hundred sixty-five words of well-being for mothers.   II. Title.

HQ759 .S63   2002
306.874'3—dc21   2002073764

1 2 3 4 5 6 7 8 9 0   LBM/LBM   1 0 9 8 7 6 5 4 3 2

ISBN 0-07-140943-2

Cover illustration by Anne Smith/www.lillarogers.com
Interior design by Jeanette Wojtyla

McGraw-Hill books are available at special quantity discounts to use as premiums
and sales promotions, or for use in corporate training programs. For more
information, please write to the Director of Special Sales, Professional Publishing,
McGraw-Hill, Two Penn Plaza, New York, NY 10121-2298. Or contact your local
bookstore.

This book is printed on acid-free paper.

For my mother, Esther, and my father, Bernard,
who always knew they had a handful.

Acknowledgments

I am grateful to God for everything.

I am grateful to my son, Ethan, and my daughter, Amara, for blessing me with the opportunity to learn what I can from this rich experience we call mothering.

I am filled with gratitude for my sweetheart, Charlie Stewart, for loving and supporting me through every single word on these pages, plus so many more that aren't quite ready for public consumption.

I am grateful to my former husband, Carl Lehrburger, for his vital role in leading me over the threshold to motherhood, and for stepping up his fathering duties so I could write this book.

The land and people of Wayne County, Utah, embraced me unconditionally while I put these words to paper, and I am especially grateful to Shirley Torgerson, Scott and Kathy Rabb, and the slick-rock canyons for their generosity and inspiring beauty.

Erin Gamble proved herself not only an incomparable mother of two, but an invaluable support preparing this manuscript.

My editor, Denise Betts, offered sustenance for both my heart and mind, and for that I am truly grateful. She will undoubtedly be a wonderful mother some day.

Introduction

I've been a mother for over sixteen years, and I think I've got the gist of it. You work, you play, you clean, you cook, you laugh, you cry, you ascend into bliss, and sometimes you crash into flames. Then, if you're lucky, you get to sleep.

Mothering is the most accelerated and intense transformational growth course ever invented. It asks you to stretch in ways you didn't even know existed. To dig deeper and open your heart wider than you ever imagined you could. To discover deeply buried treasure and untold inner resources. Most of all, mothering demands you find your own path to personal well-being while you're pulled and pushed from all directions.

These pages are a welcome companion on your journey. They're filled with words to comfort, tickle, inspire, and give you a nudge when you need to get back to center. You'll see yourself and your children on these pages. Somewhere, you'll see a bit of every mother you've ever known. Here is a rich potpourri of what it means to be a mother: the joy, the heartache, the fun, the frustration, the wadded-up tissues in your pocket, and the unending quest for a few moments alone.

This book is a friend who always understands exactly what you're going through. Keep it close by: in your purse, in your car, hung from the back of the stroller, or in your briefcase. Take it with you to the bathroom—every mother's favorite sanctuary!

Embrace these words as you will. Read them from front to back or back to front, or leap around like a bullfrog. Let the book fall open to your word for the day. Go searching for the tidbit that will remind you that there are others just like you, and that this, too, shall pass.

Savor every word and sentence this book has to offer. After all, it's all about you!

365 Words of Well-Being for Mothers

Abundance

Is there anything as big, as full, as rich and round as mothering? It all seems so huge, too large to get your arms around and too endless to even try. Blink your eyes and you are plunged into a sea of love with the power to wash you away. The responsibility is enormous. The rewards are off the charts. The nights go on for years and the days fly by at the speed of light. You suddenly need more energy and more time and more patience than you ever dreamed of—and somehow, you find it. You may not always be graceful, but you find it. You feel feelings that are deeper and sharper than any you've known, and you wonder if you will come out alive. The highs! The lows! Your plate is heaped with more sorrow and more pain and more unbridled happiness and more laughter, and like a kid in a candy store, you keep gobbling as much as you can. Whatever abundance mothering hands you, you always come out with more.

Accept

Accept the way things are. Recognize that there are some things you never will change—no matter how smart and loving you are. Accept that people will always do the best they can in that moment. Accept that if they had the capacity to do better, then surely they would. Accept a compliment graciously; don't apologize. Accept a gift with gratitude; don't push it away. Accept that your child is going through a prickly stage, and acknowledge that you have stages of your own. Know that this, too, shall pass. Your body is changing, so you'd better accept it. Accept that it will never be what it was before, and that eventually it may even be better. Accept aging without fear. Accept the fact that you can't do it all. Ask for help and accept it. Accept an invitation to get together with other mothers, and meet each one with an air of acceptance.

Agree

Move to the place where everyone can say yes. Agree on the concept if not the details. Agree that a new bike is a good idea, but not this bike at this store, and not today. Agree to pick out the right bike tomorrow. She wants television; you want a nap. Agree on quiet reading. You want pizza. He's set on Chinese. Agree to do chicken instead. Agree that the homework is a bit unreasonable, and ask him to agree that it still must be done. Agree to organize the school fund-raiser as long as they agree to try something radically new. Agree that you might have handled things with a bit more finesse. Will she agree that she jumped in too fast? Agree that it's time to redecorate the family room. Will they agree to get rid of that horrible old sofa? Agree that your ways of looking at the world are miles apart, and agree to honor those differences. When you come to a standstill, agree to disagree. When everyone agrees that the subject is closed, you can all agree on a movie.

Air

Give yourself the gift of fresh air. Breathe it in deeply, feel your belly expand, and let it out slowly. Instead of another cup of coffee, take a brisk walk in crisp autumn air to revive your senses. When cabin fever starts to suffocate you, energize yourself with a dose of frigid winter air. Feel it tickle your tongue and tingle against your tonsils. When tensions rise, step outside for a little air. Air your troubles to a friend you can trust, and clear the air of misunderstanding and mistrust. When spring lifts its head to say hello, open the windows and air out the sheets and blankets and rugs. Hang them over balconies and on clotheslines and from the branches of trees for a good soak in the sun-drenched air. Air out the cushions and the camp gear, and be certain to air out the dog. Shampoo and air-dry everybody's hair in the sun. Anything that's feeling stale and musty can benefit from a breath of fresh air. Get yourself moving and breathe!

Allow

Allow yourself to carve out a version of mothering that is totally yours. Let your road be grand and glorious, and let it be littered with stones along the way. Allow yourself to stumble, then pick yourself up, dust yourself off, and let yourself stumble again. Allow your child to make his or her own way, too. If she was born to fly, let her soar at her own speed. If he finds great joy in the pages of art books, allow his passion to feed freely and generously. Let go of what you or anyone else thinks is right for him. Simply allow him to be. Allow yourself some time and space alone. Then allow yourself some more. Grant yourself the freedom to be a sexy mother, a silly mother, a magical, mystical, musical mom. All this and more, allow.

Angels

There must be a special class of angels just for mothers. Who else could bring the blessed gift of sleep to a colicky baby and a mom on the brink of exhaustion? What magical being could pluck the lost teddy bear from the airport trash can just moments before the plane takes off? Sometimes you know it can only be angels. They show up at the last possible instant to breathe life into a newborn and give comfort to a great-grandma. Angels bring down fevers and recover kitties gone astray and help change tires on darkened highways. They watch from rooftops and park benches, and brush up against us ever so lightly to remind us that they're here. The children always see them first. Dressed in denim skirts and baseball caps and jeans with grass-stained knees, angels shovel the snow off the sidewalk, leave a casserole by the door, and carry the light of every mother's love. There are angels here just for you, mother.

Anger

Not angry, huh? That blowup in the parking lot wasn't anger? That little incident that escalated into a full-blown shouting match wasn't anger? Those feelings that start eating away at you when you're tired, stressed, hungry, and underappreciated? No anger there? Don't kid yourself. With all that you do, it's a given that you'll feel angry sooner or later. Somebody will say something that leaves a bitter taste in your mouth, and you'll spit it right back out at him or her. When anger comes knocking at your door, invite it in. Acknowledge anger as soon as it starts to spark, before it rages out of control. Before you even think of raising your hand in the direction of a child. Anger carries a sacred energy if you let it. It can clear out mountains of resentment and unexpressed frustration. It can clear the air in a minute. But first, you must name it. It's anger.

Anniversaries

If this is Tuesday, it must be the fourteenth-week anniversary of the day you all came home from the hospital. Six weeks from the first step, six hours from the last diaper, six minutes from that first boisterous "Mama." Sixteen years ago you were in labor, and now your baby is getting a driver's license! Wasn't it just four months and three Saturdays ago that you and your sweetie had a date night? And now you're doing it again! Twelve years ago you became a mother for the second time. Three and a half weeks ago, at about 4:37 P.M., you tossed out the bottles for good. But who's counting? Just a scant weekend ago your little red-haired boy rode his two-wheeler for the first time. Hard to believe now, but it was exactly seventeen months ago yesterday that you saw a picture of your new daughter and fell in love with her for the very first time. Break out the champagne! It's our anniversary! Again and again and again . . .

Anticipate

Feel it coming. Trust it's almost here. Know that everything you've worked for and dreamed about is right around the corner. **Anticipate the best** possible outcome for all. Predict that the highest good will be served. See yourself with your newborn in your arms. See the color of his eyes before they're even open. Before the kids get home from school, sense that one of them has a story she won't be pleased to share. When they ask you to guess what they're thinking, get it right. Get it right every time and anticipate they'll tell you you're psychic. **Anticipate a good report** from the orthodontist; see the braces coming off and the bill paid in full. Take your umbrella because you know it will rain. See the future unfold with joyous anticipation. Look forward to tomorrow and the riches it holds.

Arms

In a perfect world, every child would come equipped with an extra pair of arms for mom. Mothers always have so much to carry! Diaper bags and backpacks and extra sweaters and animal crackers and juice and cheese and fruit and bottles and breast pumps. Tissues and bananas and an umbrella in case it rains, books for reading and crayons for coloring, and oh, did we mention snacks? Could we please have a hand for the mothers? They navigate airports with newborns and toddler twins and nine pieces of mismatched luggage and a shoulder bag that should be put out of its misery. There she goes, lugging lawn chairs across the patio while a babe in arms squirms out of its bottom-heavy diaper. Watch her balance three paper plates, two wineglasses, a sippy cup, and a puzzle map of the United States, all the while getting stock quotes from her cell phone. Forget the roses, the candy, the moonlight. What a mother really needs is more arms!

Art

Yours, not someone else's! Your sketches, your watercolors, your poems, your songs, your bead-work, your quilting. The art that has always lived in you and isn't about to go away just because you're raising children. Your pottery, your home-made soap, your cakes, your novel, your stained glass, your carvings, your sculpture. If you have fifteen minutes a day to leaf through old maga-zines, you have fifteen minutes for your art. If you have an hour to drive to an outlet mall, you have an hour for your art. If you wait for the perfect studio, the ideal workshop, the brand-new, state-of-the-art supplies, you may never get started. If you wait for the kids to go to college, for days without interruption or months of retreat, you might never make art. Like food, air, and water, your art will sustain you. Your orchids, your needlework, your baskets, your leather. **Your expression. Your lifeblood. Your art.**

Ask

Why, oh why, is it so hard to ask? Ask for support from other nursing moms. Ask for the name of a great pediatrician who will appreciate when you ask her to go easy on the antibiotics. Ask someone to help you with the kids on the days you have meetings in town. No request is too outrageous or too stupid to ask. Just raise your hand and ask. When you need it, ask everybody you know for help. Ask friends. Ask family. Ask your God. Ask the local department store to install baby-changing stations. Ask your mother-in-law to crochet one of her precious afghans. Go ahead and ask them to let you live in the house rent-free. What's the harm if you ask? When you want to know the answers, come right out and ask. You'll never get what you want if you're too shy to ask.

Awareness

Cultivate greater awareness. Wake up enough to know that things are not as simple as they seem. Develop a deeper understanding of your own patterns and issues. Become aware of your standard operating procedures, of the predictable ways you hide your feelings and relive old hurts again and again. Could your frustration with your daughter be related to your dissatisfaction at work? Duh! Is all the angst and crying really about who does the dishes—or are you feeling undervalued and unappreciated? Duh! Are you blaming your teenager for breaking his curfew because your boundaries are the ones that need setting? Double duh! Awareness is the first step to greater self-knowledge. Once you are more conscious of the larger picture, you can focus on making changes. Awareness takes you right up to insight. Then your "Duh!" becomes your "Aha!"

Baby-Sitters

If mothers had their say, baby-sitters would have their own Hall of Fame. There's Marie, who drove four hours in a snowstorm because she knew you couldn't miss your big meeting. Gonzalo, who spent half a day coaxing Gilbert out of a tree and the other half holding the frightened kitten in a blanket on his lap. And who could forget Amelia, who sang your colicky infant to sleep while putting out that small fire behind the garage? A good baby-sitter is worth whatever you pay her—and probably a great deal more. He knows how to make "ants on a log" and will play fifty-two-card pickup for hours. She'll turn off the VCR and tell politically correct fairy tales using puppets she crocheted out of string. The best baby-sitters, you'll never forget. The worst ones, you can't even remember their names!

Bags

This big one is full of old clothes that you've been meaning to donate for years. That one on the shelf in the garage is crammed to the top with yogurt cups to recycle. Over here is a garbage bag stuffed with old pantyhose that surely must be useful! The canvas bag just inside the back door has sand toys, sunscreen, two towels, and a beach pass. Here's the plastic shopping bag that went to the slumber party filled with snacks and extra clothing, and came back completely empty. On the chair in the bedroom is the bag you'll take with you to the hospital. Right alongside is the zipper bag filled with diapers and flannel blankets for the trip back home. Why hasn't this bag of frozen groceries been put away? Whose gym bag is that on the table? For all of the bags you keep schlepping around, the ones you can't lift are right under your eyes.

Balance

Face it! Mothering is one never-ending balancing act, performed under the bright lights in the center ring. Work. Play. Self. Others. Give. Receive. All. Nothing. In all things, find your center. In all ways, find the balance. Woman. Mother. Daughter. Wife. Inner. Outer. When you tip too far in one direction, find your center. Find your balance. When the teeter starts to totter, plant both feet firmly on the ground and find balance within. Too much. Not enough. Too strict. Too laid-back. Too loud. Invisible. Over-aggressive. A doormat. In between the extremes, find the place you call balance. When the swing settles down, feel the balance begin. The moment you feel that you're losing your balance, slow down, unclench your jaw, then seek balance again.

Bananas

Bravo for bananas! In lunchrooms and playgrounds all over the world, bananas take center stage at snack time. They nestle next to peanut butter and honey and fit perfectly into little hands and come with their own recyclable skin. Banana and jelly on rice cake? Divine! You can dip them into chocolate and smash them into mash and teeth are never required. They're fabulous frozen. Stupendous in smoothies. Perfect in pudding, they're paradise in pies. And ten out of ten smart mothers agree: when the cupboard is bare, bananas always round out a marginal meal. A mother feeding her child a banana in public will never be accosted by a nosy stranger impersonating the health food police. You can peel me a grape or peel me some shrimp, but bananas are the fruit that appeals to moms most. And that includes moms who are monkeys.

Bare

Now and then it's good to bare your soul. You can spill your guts and strip away the excess and get to the bones of the matter. Once in a while it's good to get back to the bare essentials. To trim away the excess that's starting to smother you, and start over with a bare piece of ground and a song in your heart. Childhood is the time to run around bare naked in the back, so let them have their fun—with bare feet, to boot. Let your little girl go bare-breasted while the only thing that's round and soft is her tummy. Put your foot down when her older sister wants to parade around with a bikini that's barely there. After your hair falls out, buy beautiful scarves to wear. Later when you're ready, be brave and go bare. Watch out when a handful of hungry teenage boys drop by for dinner. When the party is over, your cupboard will be bare.

Bathe

When you can, fill the tub with hot water and bathe. Add two drops of lavender oil, turn off the lights and bring out the candles, and soak yourself into blissful oblivion. Let your bath be your own private ritual, your most sacred sanctuary. Bathe away anything the day has left behind. Bathe away the regret for losing your temper, the guilt for not getting to the school play before the third act, the stress from staying late at work and missing family dinner. Let the waters renew you and replenish your peace. Float in an unending sea, a crystalline mountain lake, an ancient ceremonial bath offered only to mothers. Feel the water caress your skin as you lovingly lather every inch of your body. When done, towel dry and roll into bed where your dreams can bathe you anew.

Be

Be yourself first, a woman second, and a mother third. Be every bit of who you are. Be serious, be focused, be reliable. Be silly, be carefree, be wildly unpredictable. Be all you've ever believed yourself to be—and then be more. Be willing to be a lot more than you ever thought you could be. Be more creative, more expressive, more loving, more sexual. Be happy. Be sad. Be angry and rageful and sometimes, yes, be afraid. Be the mother you always wished you had. Be the mother you always knew you were destined to be. Be punctual or be late. Be ready or be disorganized. Be there or be square. Allow yourself to be your authentic self; let your spirit be all it can be. Show your kids what it's like to be a full-spectrum human being. Model for them how real life can be. Then be quiet, be still, and just let them be.

Beauty

Do you know how beautiful you are? Do you see that love pours out of your eyes and your heart radiates so that you positively glow? Beauty surrounds you through every stage of mothering. When you're pregnant. When you're nursing. When you're chasing a runaway toddler through the museum. When you're walking down the street with your eighteen-year-old. When you play in the park with your grandchild. You're beautiful when you're curled up on the sofa in your favorite blankie, too tired to even get up. Your tears and your sorrow are filled with beauty; you're a wonder of grace under fire. You're beautiful when you fight for what you know is important and you don't budge an inch from the truth. You handle your affairs with a quiet beauty. There's a beauty in the way you're living your life, and it's a beautiful sight to behold.

Beginnings

There was an old woman who swallowed a fly.
Once upon a time, in a kingdom far away, lived a
generous king and a beautiful princess. Before
you were born, your father and I met at church in
a small town in Kentucky. Down by the banks of
the hanky-panky, a bullfrog jumped from bank to
banky. When your grandparents were still teenagers, their families left everything they had and
traveled to a strange new country. Long, long ago,
longer than you can imagine, people lived on the
land and were guided by the stars. When I was
just about your age, I wanted a puppy more than
anything in the world. When two people love
each other very much, they can make a baby in a
most beautiful way. When the trains used to
come through here three times a day, your uncle
and I would run to the top of the hill to wave at
the engineer.

In the beginning . . .

Believe

What you believe is what your life will be. So believe that which you truly desire. Believe that this phase will pass and so will every one that follows. Believe your instincts. When your heart tells you your child must go to a particular school or a particular doctor, trust the wisdom of your heart against all else. If they tell you everything is fine and you feel otherwise, believe your intuition and ask others to believe it, too. Believe the truth, even when it's hard or painful or nearly impossible to believe. When your child says, "I'm scared," believe him. When she says, "I don't feel good," believe it. When your teenager swears she wasn't at the party, believe her because she is who you believe her to be. What you choose to believe is the life you create. Choose carefully what you believe.

Birds

Blessings on you if you live near the birds! These high-flying creatures remind us of the power of spreading our wings. Birds know their place in the circle of life and never strive to be anything different. They feather their nests with the hunk of hair your daughter cleaned out of her hairbrush, and the lint that escaped through your dryer vent. If you ever feel that mealtime is never-ending, watch a mother robin return time and again to drop worms into the gaping beaks of birdlings. Let your heart soar at the sight of birds. A hawk circling above an open valley. The bright yellow meadowlark singing his cheery song. The stately swan who all but slides over the water while paddling furiously below. Bring birds out of the background and off the pages of books. Invite them into your backyard with bird-baths and feeders. Visit them at the aviary, stop the car to watch their aerial antics, and discover them in places you thought they deserted. Turn your eyes to the heavens, the trees, and the gardens. It's worth looking out for the birds.

Birth

The birth of a mother is a wonder to see. The air
is ripe with creation, filled with anticipation and
the promise of new life. Perhaps it is the child
who gives birth to the mother, carrying her over
the threshold on soft pink soles and wings of
delight. It is arduous work, a woman's journey
into motherhood. She grunts and moans and
writhes and wonders how such a thing can
possibly be. She cries and opens herself deeply to
enter a world that only mothers know. And how
she is welcomed on arrival! We wrap her in warm
blankets and wipe sweat from her brow, while
grace holds the room in the palm of her hand. A
hush of voices, a whispered prayer, sweet
murmurs, and kisses on her forehead. The miracle
astounds us, enwraps us with joy, every moment a
mother is born.

Blend

Life as a mother is a rich stew of farm-fresh, gourmet ingredients mixed with yesterday's leftovers and a few handfuls of the unknown. It's a blend of sweet and savory, sorrow and joy, pain and pleasure, and a pinch of something that you can't even name. You're blending siblings and steps, fathers and lovers, children and grownups, three snakes and a ferret, and most of the time it just simmers. You're a chef extraordinaire, blending work and home and trying to keep it all from turning to slop. Mothering is a blend of art and science, magic and miracles, temperament and talent. You need heart and head in a two-to-one ratio, a sack of courage, and patience by the pound. Too much of anything and the flavors won't marry. Too much of nothing and nothing ever gels. A life of extremes offers potent polarities. Right in the middle is the best of all blends.

Blessings

Count them! You're blessed with good health, good life, good friends. You're blessed to live in a place where you can speak your mind and not be carried off in shackles. You've been blessed with a child or with children—no matter how they came to you and no matter how long they stay. What a blessing is your ear for music! How blessed you are with a capable mind! You share the blessings of your heart every day, and to others, you're surely a blessing. Your refrigerator is filled and your home is dry and every step that you take has been blessed. What blessings upon you have been made! The woman on the sidewalk who asks you for change is a blessing that reminds you of your riches. You're blessed each morning with a brand-new beginning and blessed with the free will to shape it. You can spend a lifetime lamenting all that you lack. Wouldn't you rather be counting your blessings?

Blossom

You never see the moment it happens. You wait and you watch, and one day, life stirs in delicious new ways. You spy a tiny crocus pushing its way through the snow. You stop doubting yourself as a parent, and you feel the quickening of a new confidence within. Everything blossoms in its own time, in its own way. Just like your baby. When you least expect it, she starts singing her very own song. You quietly enter the room, and there's your little one, discovering that his hands can dance. Something new and unexpected is emerging, and you find yourself living with a raucous comedian. Or a charmer. Or an intensely quiet observer. You'll never capture the precise moment of your child's unfolding. Nor of your own. It's a never-ending show of indefinable wonder. Bright and beautiful as a rose in bloom, and unlike anything else in the garden.

Books

I don't remember a single time that my mom
wasn't reading a book. She'd come home from the
library with canvas bags filled with mysteries and
histories and books about building adobe houses
and designing heirloom quilts. They always sat in
piles on the floor and the counter and the table
beside her favorite reading chair. Who knows how
many she actually read? Every time we looked,
there was a new batch. Some she bought so she
could take them into the bathtub. When someone
wanted her, she'd call out, "One more chapter!"
and then she'd be gone for another hour or two.
We could always tell what was up with Mom by
the books she was reading. When she couldn't put
down *Women Who Run with the Wolves*, we knew
things were about to change. When the low-fat,
low-cholesterol cookbooks appeared, it was a sure
sign we would soon be eating tofu. I think you
could say that all of those years, Mom was having
an affair with her books.

Boundaries

It's easy for a mother to lose sight of her boundaries. Where do you begin and others leave off? Where do you draw the line at giving—and how wide do you open the gates to receive? Boundaries aren't meant to be barbed-wire fences and heavy steel doors that lock out all who would prey upon you. They're simply markers that help you define how far out your edges go, and how closely others can approach you. If you don't clearly post your boundaries, how can others know if they're trampling them? Healthy boundaries are fluid, moving and dancing around you. Like an empress living in a castle, you can raise and lower the gates as you wish. A little higher to foster greater intimacy; lower when things are feeling too close for comfort. Create boundaries before others create them for you. Only you are the keeper; only you hold the keys.

Breaks

You deserve a handful! How about that big break you've been waiting for since long before the kids arrived? For now, you're satisfied with little breaks throughout the day: chai on the house. Ten minutes of chair massage. A remarkable show of compassion by a stranger. Give yourself a break. Lighten up on the self-criticism and the constant second-guessing. Take yourself out for a lunch you know won't break the bank. (Don't take the baby or you might break some dishes.) Will this stormy weather ever break? When spring break rolls around, make a break for some warm southern sunshine. Take a break from the busyness of every day and gently break into meditation. Break that endless loop of internal chatter that spins around and around in your mind like a broken record. It's a self-defeating pattern that you'll surely want to break.

Breakthrough

After months of wrestling with an impossible question, suddenly you're hit with the answer. You give up all hope of figuring things out, and presto! It takes care of itself. You can break through old habits in the blink of an eye, after gaining awareness for decades. After lifetimes of banging on doors that won't open, you suddenly realize the door is not there. What looks like a breakdown is really a breakthrough. Walls that littered your way disappear. Foundations you stood on collapse underneath you, and your tumble takes you straight into breakthrough. A baby can teeth in delirious pain until his gum is ready for breakthrough. The paperwork sits without moving for ages and then something cracks and there's breakthrough. You can build a stone tower to lock up your emotions, until you discover that all along you've held the key. Then it's easy to step out and break through.

Brush

Brush your finger oh-so gently across your baby's cheek and feel your breath taken away by the absolute softness. Brush that silky fine hair with that soft brush and blow on that little curl and watch it dance in the wind. Brush your daughter's hair until it glistens in the sun, then brush it into kinky pigtails tied up in satin ribbon. When your tears slip out of your eyes at the piano recital or the basketball game or when the children's choir sings, brush them away before they slide off the end of your chin. Brush your teeth after every meal, and teach your children to do the same. On your way home from work, pick up a new paintbrush and some watercolors and brush away the cares of the day.

Call

Call me when you get there, honey. Call me when you leave. If you get into trouble, call me. If you need a ride, call me. You can always call your mother. Call anytime, day or night. Why didn't you call me sooner? Call as soon as you get the results after the tryouts, and tell me how you did. Or tell me how you didn't. Hey dude, the police are here and I think it's time to call your mother. Call collect if you have to. It might be your last chance to call. The minutes are free; why not call Mom? Call when it's Mother's Day and especially when it's not. I think it's time to call the doctor. Did you remember to call the sitter? I promise to keep the phone turned on all night. This is one call a mother won't want to miss.

Can

Yes, you can! You can be a mother and a lover and a goddess all rolled into one. You can spend time with your children and time with your dreams and still get a decent night's sleep. Can you tend to your own needs and care for your children, too? You can! Can a thirty-eight-year-old mother of three run a marathon and beat her own mother? You bet you can! Can you get a college degree over the Internet while your little one's napping? Can you wear something slinky when everyone else is going sensible? Can you make it through another year of diapers and runny noses? Yes, you can! Yes, you can! Yes, you can! You can be the best mother in the world while you build your career. You can stay full-time at home and keep your edge in the market.

Let them tell you you can't, then just answer, "I can! Yes, I can! Yes, I can! Yes, I can!"

Candlelight

Candles cast a light all their own. The flames flicker and dance with the slightest movement, and paint fanciful shadows on plain white walls. Candlelight transports us to ancient stone chambers and medieval castles and reflects a long ago, simpler time. They soften everything and lay a blanket of quiet over a nerve-wracking day. In the light of a candle, faces lose their grip and eyes sparkle. Everyone becomes more beautiful in the pale golden glow. People move closer to one another. Voices lower and gestures lose their edge. In a room lit by candles, the television and computer seem loudly out of place. Candlelight slows us down and helps us draw peace from the darkness. We read at a leisurely pace and speak of unhurried things. A candle was born to burn far beyond birthdays. "Shhh, Mom is lighting the candles again."

Catch

If you run really fast, you can catch the 7:15
show. Or you can skip the whole thing and catch
a catnap before bed. Then maybe you won't catch
that bug that the whole house has already caught.
If you push yourself right over the edge, you
might be able to catch up on your work. Or you
can forget about it and go catch fireflies instead.
You can try again and again to catch flies with
vinegar, until you finally wise up and bring out
the honey. Remember when your little baseball
player was learning to catch for the very first
time? You positioned the hands just so, sides of
the palms butted up against each other and the
whole arrangement stuck to her tummy with
invisible glue. You said, "Just stand there and wait
with your hands open, and the ball will drop right
in." You can catch a lot that way. Peel your
clenched fingers apart. Open your palms so you're
set to receive. Then patiently wait for your catch
to come in.

Celebrate

Oh, go on and have a party for absolutely any reason. Or better yet, for no reason at all. First tooth? Celebrate! Last day of preschool? Celebrate! Third time in two weeks that the cat left hairballs outside the bathroom? Celebrate! Blow up balloons and paint stars and hearts on everybody's cheeks. Dig into ice cream before noon and don't you dare check the nutritional statement on the side of the container. When you make it through another night with a newborn or another week with a toddler or another month with a girl who seems ten going on eighteen, you deserve a celebration. Don't wait for the calendar to tell you when it's a special occasion.

Anytime's the right time for celebration.

Center

You can always find your way back to center. It's there, buried under the mountain of laundry and the leftover dishes and the piles of unfinished projects and little (and big) voices that never stop calling. Your job is to make your way back to center. Take a ten-minute walk. Lie down in a quiet room or on a patch of ground. Do something to move deeper into your body. Dance. Run. Swim. Move some blocked energy. Write. Draw. Sew. Knit. Check in: are you breathing? Ponder or pray or simply sit in silent reflection. Eat something real! Bread. Turkey. Cheese. Eggs. Peanut butter on toast. Do one small task that matters to you. Call back your best friend. Send a card. Take a bath, a shower, a nap. Listen to classical music. Read inspiring words. Sweep. Garden. Vacuum. Build something. It's not so much what you do, but how and why you do it. A thousand roads will lead you to your center, but only if you choose one to take.

Challenge

Challenge is the fertilizer that fosters your growth. Sometimes it feels like handfuls of manure being flung in your face, but oh, what blossoms it brings! Every challenge tempers you with an interior strength and grace. Every obstacle pushes you to find another way, forge another path, create a brand-new solution. Every challenge you overcome is a victory of spirit. Every challenge you face is a call to summon up more of the good stuff and put it to the highest use you can muster. Don't remove challenge from the path of your child and don't curse it when it calls your name. Without challenge, you remain soft and mushy around the edges. You miss the opportunity to transform thorns into peacock feathers and sand into pearls. Like the chisel that releases an image from stone, challenge is a tool that invites you to use it. Accept the offer and make your challenges your own.

Chaos

It's absolute bedlam! Pandemonium reigns! The
phone is ringing and your teenager is screeching!
The dryer is buzzing, the microwave beeping, and
the television is turned up to the max! The
kitchen table is littered with dishes! Every plate,
bowl, and cup is down from the shelf! The puppy
is devouring your favorite slipper! The cat is
carving up your favorite door! Your daughter is
dancing on the back of the sofa! She's spreading
confetti all over the floor! Someone is crying in
the bathroom! Mom's final drawings are covered
with corn! The dishwasher's overflowing! There's
soap in the hall! The baby's nose is bleeding!
What's that noise? It's the fax machine faxing!
What's that truck in the driveway? They're
cleaning the drains! The noise! The confusion! It's
utterly mad! The most wonderful chaos you've
ever had!

Chocolate

Gotta have chocolate. With nuts or without. Bite-sized or in fist-sized chunks, in boxes or bags or wrapped in beautiful paper by a handsome chocolatier. Fudge will do. Long-eared bunnies will do. Jelly beans? Won't do. Just about anything homemade will definitely do. Chips out of the bag, uh-huh, if you can find them stashed in the back of the freezer. Sweet, dark, drinkable. Milk, mocha, munchable. A mother can go for days on chocolate she can call her own. Just this once, you get it all. Just this time, you don't need to share. Savor every lick, every nibble, every sweet morsel of delectable delight. Gobble up the whole thing or ration it to last the night. Okay, maybe to last the hour. Count on your hormones to call in every ounce of chocolate within miles. Every mom with a sweet tooth will tell you the rule: Don't come between me and my chocolate!

Choice

In every moment, the choice is yours. You choose to move forward or back off. To be the parent or the friend. To call the doctor or ride out the fever. You choose to see a problem or an opportunity. You decide what values to pass along to your children, and when they're older, it's their choice whether to keep them. Make your choice: will you react in anger or respond with creative solutions? You choose: will you surround your child with firm boundaries to bump up against or will you simply hope she'll come up with her own? Every moment you can make healthy choices for yourself: Herbal tea instead of another cup of coffee. A crisp green salad over deep-fried fast foods. A half-hour walking or dancing or reading, rather than thirty minutes on the phone with someone you don't even like. Choose love, not fear. Choose acceptance, not judgment. Choose unity over separation. What will you teach your child today? Think it through wisely. The choice is always yours.

Circles

Nothing about mothering goes in a straight line, so it's good to get acquainted with circles. Not the kind that keep you chasing your tail day after day, but the ones that remind us there are no beginnings and no ends. Like the circle of giving and receiving, which flows freely as long as no strings become tangled. The circle of life, death, and rebirth that is at the root of all nature and the core of every life. Step out of linear thinking that moves directly from Point A to Point B, and discover a circular logic. Enter the labyrinth at the edge of the city and find your answers in a circular path. Everything that goes around, comes around; embrace the full circle that it brings. When you think you've been crowned the queen of the world, look around, you're just one in the circle. Unlike a pyramid with a top and a bottom, there's no above, no below, in the circle.

Clarity

As soon as you know what you're about, everything about you becomes crystal-clear. Dig your way through the murky confusion until clarity shines through the clouds. Start weeding out what you don't want, and then sure as the sun rises in the east, you'll be clear about what you desire. Clarity is catching. Like kindness and respect, it passes from person to person in a continual chain. Seek clarity around your style of discipline, and your daughter will get it without any questions. Firm up your standards for personal grooming, and help guide your son toward clarifying his. When others detect your clarity, they want to have some of their own. Clarity arrives when it's ready, and can never be forced. If you're not clear on an issue, just let it ride unanswered. When clarity emerges, you'll know clearly where you stand.

Clean

Clarity comes easier when things are clean.
Instead of looking at cleaning as endless drudgery,
embrace it as a meditation. You're cleaning the
mirror so you can get a better look at how others
see you. You're cleaning the counters to give yourself space to write, to sew, to draw, without
bumping into distractions no matter which way
you turn. Cleaning out the attic is a first step
toward discarding old furniture from an old
marriage, and dumping old habits that no longer
fit your design for living. When you remove the
streaks and stains from your windows, you shine
up every facet of your personal vision. You can
spend hours cleaning out the space under the
porch, raking up the remains of old life and dead
dreams. Feel yourself stretch while you vacuum.
Sway with the rhythm of sweeping. Wipe away
the layers that obscure your brilliance. Dust yourself off and wipe your slate clean.

Click

You meet another mom and you instantly click.
The kids play together and again, there's a click.
You find a new town and everything clicks. You
meet your pediatrician for the very first time and,
thanks to small favors, you click. Click! You find a
source of your favorite (and rare) toffee crunchies.
Click! You stop a stranger to ask the time and
click! it's your high school math teacher. Your
long-lost uncle moves in for a while, and to
everyone's relief, it's a click. You host a dinner
party and the tablemates click. You set up a blind
date. Can you believe it? They click! A new baby-
sitter and it's one awesome click. You sign up for
aerobics. The class is a click! The first time your
eyes met, you were stunned by the click. Click!
You've got children! How could they not click?

Climb

No matter how deep the pit you've fallen into,
you can always make your way to the top. You
can put one hand in front of the other and take
hold of whatever sturdy branch or stone or
helping hand you can grab. You can get ahead
making tiny baby steps, one after another, inching
your way up a steep incline. You might slip back
two steps for every three you take, yet you must
continue to climb. Sometimes we fall into the
same hole over and over again, until we learn to
walk down a different road. Call for help if you
must. Toss anything you have out of the hole to
get the attention of passersby. Deep holes can
appear throughout a mother's life. Call them
depression. Call them isolation. Call them cabin
fever or hormones or low blood-sugar. Anytime
you find yourself in a dark muddy hole,
remember there's a way to climb out.

Closed

You can't be eternally open. There comes a time to close the gate, to bar the door, and to protect yourself from intrusion. It doesn't mean that you've shut down for good. For now, you just can't stay open. You might be in a fragile space of your own; other-focused or maybe just tired. Put out the sign that says "Closed" and hope that others will notice. It's okay for a mom's bedroom door to be closed. It's okay to close the kitchen sometime after ten. You can give yourself permission not to leave your heart standing wide open and exposed. You can choose not to bare your soul to all who will knock. Once in a while, you can turn down your willingness to listen to everyone's opinion and endlessly process. Now and again, you can say you're not open and they can try someone else. The first several times you will meet with resistance. End of discussion. The subject is closed.

Collapse

When the nights are too short and the days too
harried, you really must collapse. Give it all up for
an hour or two or more and refuse to hold it all
together any longer. Let gravity take its course.
Collapse into the arms of someone who loves you.
Collapse on the floor with a pillow, with your
softest blankie, and cry until your eyes are red
and swollen and all cried out. Ask someone else to
be with the children. Ask someone else to make
the dinner, do the laundry, organize the bake sale,
tend the garden, watch the restaurant, circulate
the draft report for comments. Ask as you hope
they would someday ask you. And when they say
yes, climb into bed or slip into the tub or lie
down on a soft patch of ground. Sometimes you
can only collapse. Breathe deep, ask for help.
Then collapse.

Collect

Seashells. Coins. Stamps. Stickers. Angels perched upon glass shelves. Mushrooms. Old keys. Linen doilies. Ruddy-cheeked ceramic elves. Magazines from 1900. Matchbooks. Chapbooks. Silver spoons. Money from foreign nations. Papyrus rubbings from ancient tombs. Crystals. China. Tiny foxes. Mason jars and music boxes. Handmade paper. Fountain pens. Windup toys and dolls that bend. Whalebone corsets. Ocean shots. Miniature fruit arranged in pots. Olympic pins. All kinds of hearts. Imported pans for pies and tarts. Handblown glass. Pepper grinders. Rusty locks from old wood doors. All things Elvis. Green silk scarves. No matter what I have, I keep collecting more.

Color

Feeling kind of monotone? Get yourself a new box of crayons and a new set of paints and lose yourself in rainbows of color. Color between the lines and outside the lines and right over the lines if you like. Color is a magical potion that can transform anything into nearly anything else! Feeling blah in the bedroom? Add rich, deep, sensuous colors, romantic and sizzling and warm. Kids bouncing off the walls? Trade in those bright, hot hues for soothing nature tones. Paint an entire room white and then drape splashes of color and hang starbursts of color and next Tuesday, color it all over again. Feeling stressed? Replace those active, productive, hungry reds with violet and lavender that raise your inner vibration and support greater balance. Color can lift you out of sorrow, expand your horizons, and heal old hurts. Wander through paint stores, play with watercolors, and feel your way through fabrics. Look past your eyes and see color.

Come

Come to a new place of understanding. Come for a week and stay for a lifetime. Come by yourself and the rest of the family will follow. Come to a startling new realization that the kind of mothering that brings you the greatest joy is the best you can bring to your children. Come out of whatever closet you've locked yourself into. Come out smiling. Let the past come to an obvious conclusion and let a fresh perspective come shining through. Invite all your friends to a backyard barbecue and see who comes through the gate. Don't worry; your daughter will come to her senses and come clean with the truth. Eventually, they'll all come around. Come to a crossroads and look both ways to see what's coming. Come to an agreement that serves the party of the first part and the party of the second part equally well. Know that in time, everything will come 'round full circle.

Commit

Commit to the dance, but not the steps. Your commitment to love your child unconditionally may take different forms as the years go by. The primary commitment never wavers. Your commitment to your creativity might mean secluding yourself as an artist for a time, or teaching in a public school. What remains consistent is your core commitment. Nothing can transcend your commitment to yourself and your own well-being. No contract, no signed paper, no agreement will supersede your commitment to your God. Commit to listening to your inner guidance. Commit to speaking your authentic truth. Commit to believing in the goodness of life no matter what trials may befall you. Commit to the dance of relationship—and know that what begins as a tango may shift to a waltz and eventually end up a ballet. What matters is your commitment to dance. The steps can change come what may.

Community

Create the village that will help raise the children. Connect with other mothers because you live nearby, because you work the same schedules, because your children connected in a lovely way at the park. Or just because you smiled at each other in that knowing woman's way. Come together as a community where everyone can ask for support and know that it will be offered. Create community around shared values, common spiritual directions, or because you're attracted to a culture and outlook profoundly different from your own. Go beyond what you imagine your community to be. Break out of old communities that no longer serve you and move into communities where every experience is honored. Build a virtual community or a physical community or a community of the heart. When you find your true community, you will know without doubt you are home.

Compassion

Accept every moment with compassion. In the midst of self-doubt, seek a way to lighten up and give yourself a break. Acknowledge that you are human and you're doing the best you can. Offer yourself some compassion. When you feel a slide into judgment and blame, switch over and bring up compassion. Find a place in your deepest heart for those who seem easiest to judge. Practice compassion in all things. Make it a discipline and commit yourself to learning compassion. Walk away from an argument with compassion for those you can't agree with. In the midst of untold suffering, call up a tenderness for everyone involved. Forgive the driver who angrily cut you off at the stop sign. Send some compassion his way. Withhold judgment of the mother whose children are in trouble. Imagine the pain that is troubling her, too. An opening heart and radiant love are powerful tools of compassion.

Completion

Sometimes you're just done and you know it. You're finished. It's time to turn the page and get on to the next chapter. You're like a chick in an egg that's suddenly too cramped and dark and stifling, and you must start chipping your way out. It's as if you've grown too large for your own story and you're bursting at all kinds of seams. You can be humming along in a job you enjoy and suddenly, like a bolt out of the blue, you know that it's over. You can dearly love every moment of being a stay-at-home mom, and one day you wake up and it's over. Time for the next phase. Time to begin a new cycle. There's nothing wrong. It's not a problem. You've just completed whatever you set out to do and sticking around any longer will only keep you in a box you've outgrown. Learn to acknowledge endings as the natural evolutions that they are, and honor the fullness of completion. Then you can move with grace and ease into the joy of brand-new beginnings.

Concede

Admit that you might have done better. Acknowledge that you meant well, but it wasn't quite enough. Give a gracious concession speech. Concede that your idea for a children's museum may have been a bit overzealous. Concede that something quieter is more of a fit. Recognize that you're a good woman, but maybe not the best one for the job this time. Congratulate the winner and let it go with grace. Teach your children that when you concede the race, you don't agree that you're a loser—only that somebody else won this time. Concede that your strawberry-rhubarb pie was a little too tart to take the blue ribbon. Accept the decision of the judges or the fates and just leave it at that. Let it go and let someone else reap the glory. You may have come close, but someone else hit the mark.

Confirmation

Wonderful things happen when you're on the right track. Confirmation shows up from the most interesting sources. Synchronicity takes center stage at every turn. You're thinking about making a move, and within days a town, a house, and people who feel like they're already friends practically fall from the sky into your lap. You're wondering if your child should transfer to a different school, and through no action on your part, a flyer appears in the mail. You're looking for a book club and the one night you stop by the bookstore after work, they're meeting to discuss the book you came to buy. Your intuition tells you you're getting close to a long-held goal, and all of a sudden, the time, the space, and the money you need are yours with little to no effort. You can solicit feedback and seek confirmation, but why bother? When your heart guides you and you're walking your truth, the universe will shower you with abundant confirmation.

Connect

Experience the ease of connecting. Don't rush around town looking for the right group or the right place or the perfect circle. Don't wind yourself up worrying about memberships and dues and bylaws and meeting schedules. Just let yourself know that you're ready to connect with other mothers. Allow that you would enjoy linking up with a mom who thinks about mothering the same way you do. Who can hear you in a way that no one else can. Who has a little more experience, perhaps. Or a little less. Connect with single moms or coupled moms; hook up with moms who know moms who, of course, know other moms. Connections happen in extraordinary ways when you let them. In the ladies' bathroom at the department store. When your strollers get tangled at the entrance to the gym. Over a perfectly ripe pineapple at the farmers' market. Be the kind of mom you'd love to connect with, then watch how easy it is to connect.

Contentment

Contentment invites you to be at peace with what is. It's more subtle than happiness, more grounded than rapture, and accessible every moment. Contentment tells you that you have enough and you are enough and that it's good. When you're content, you rest in what is, instead of racing after what should be. When you find contentment, you still have dreams, but the difference is that they don't have you. Right now, are you content? Do you feel present and complete with what this moment provides? Can you savor the apple in your hand, take delight in the child at your side, and appreciate all that surrounds you—without wondering if there's something better? Can you survey your world and feel the calm of contentment? Can you let yourself bask without reaching for more? Contentment never asks you to settle for less, simply to acknowledge there's enough in what there is now.

Contrast

Sometimes when you're wobbling with indecision, life presents you with such startling contrasts that everything snaps into focus. You observe a mother so serene with her child that at once you strengthen your resolve to heal your anger. A harsh exchange unfolds before you in a shopping mall, and in that moment you know you'll do everything to steer clear of that path. Contrasts take us to extremes so we can find our way back to balance. You may have to go further in one direction than you thought possible, to understand that you never want to return there again. Once you come face to face with hatred, you know your only choice is love. Once war reaches out and touches you, you will never again question the power of peace. You wonder whether staying at home is worth it, and once you spend time with a latchkey child, your doubt disappears. Contrasts offer a wonderful opportunity: only after you are shown what you cannot tolerate, will you create what you truly desire.

Conversation

You're starving for close conversation of the adult kind. You want an opening question more intellectually stimulating than "What sound does the pig make?" You're not an elitist, but you could surely enjoy conversing with someone who has more than a second-grade education. You're aching to talk with another human being, not just at them. Your hunger for vocabulary is voracious. Your quest for a long session of loquaciousness just won't quit. What you wouldn't give to babble on about Brazil! What joy you would find to expound on extraterrestrials, and elicit a response that goes beyond "Whatever." You're ready to talk long into the night, to share meaningful discourse for hours on end. An intimate discussion on the filmmaker's art would drive you to rare heights of passion. If worse comes to worse, you can talk to yourself—but it won't feed your craving for deep conversation.

Courage

A mother's courage is a powerful force. It is the courage that rises up and declares to the experts, "This child will not be left behind." It is courage borne out of love and tempered by the heart's own song. What courage lives in a woman who carries a child of uncertain capacity! How courageous the mother who flees in the night to lead her children to safety and shelter! A mother's brave heart will drive her to battle unthinkable odds on behalf of her offspring. She will lasso heaven and earth and move mountains to ensure that her child gets all he deserves. She will stand her ground in the face of relentless opposition and garner every resource to advance her cause. Her motherly might will topple laws and corporations, and serve as a beacon for mothers to come. When she's infused with love and on fire with courage, a battle against a mother will never be won.

Create

Keep those juices flowing! Let the muse visit you often, and enrich the world with your creativity. Create with pen and ink, with paper, with clay, with paint, with fabric, food, and flowers. Keep it simple. Make up new games, new meals, new ways to bring balance into every day. Start with a big, beautiful pile of nothing and create! Create a playroom out of old scarves and pillows until you're inspired to create something else with a can of paint, three pieces of wood, and a shoebox filled with ribbons and buttons. Create a butterfly garden where there was once a pile of dead brush. Create a home infused with love and comfort. Think you're not the creative type? You have the power to create life for another. Now take that creative power and create a life of your own!

Cross

Cross every bridge you come to and be thankful you don't have to ford the river with a team of wild horses. If you get to a rough crossing where there is no bridge, use your wits to create one of your own. Never burn a bridge that you might want to cross back over at another time. Create a rite of passage when your daughter crosses the bridge into womanhood. Gather a cross-section of friends and family and women of all ages. Honor, too, your son's crossing. Blend traditions that have for centuries marked such a step for a man with a journey, a test, a prayer. Foster your family's love of reading and writing with crossword puzzles every day. (When you're stumped, try not to utter a string of cross words!) When you need to be firm, draw a line in the sand and suggest very strongly that no one cross over it. Instead of flying coast-to-coast, try crisscrossing the country. Stop for a piece of pie in every state that you cross.

Crush

When I was about twelve, my mom had the biggest crush on my brother. He was sixteen and playing ball, dark as a berry with a smile that lit up the room. He was a good guy and had lots of friends, but his grades weren't always the best. He was working out at the gym every day, and liked to wear tight shirts and show everybody his six-pack. Don't get me wrong; Mom wasn't weird or gross about it or anything. She just thought he was so totally cool. She went to every single one of his games and always yelled the loudest. When he made points for the team, the other moms would cry out, "That's your boy!" and she always got tears in her eyes. Sometimes I really hated him, because he was so annoying. But I have to admit, I had a crush on him, too.

Cry

Cry the tears only a mother can cry. Tears of joy, tears of sorrow, tears you held inside all those years when you never, ever would let them see you cry. Let the tears fall, slowly escaping from sodden eyes. Let them wash over your face in great sheets, pouring out and washing clean your driest inner spaces. Cry for your newborn who made it through a rough night. Or didn't. Cry when your middle-born sings the solo, makes the goal, tells the truth, does the laundry, stands up for compassion, writes you a poem. Cry for your first child, your last child, and the child you barely got to know. Cry for your own changing body. Grieve the loss of that which is no more and weep for joy at that which is only now unfolding. Know that when rain falls from above, an angel sheds tears for a mother.

Dance

If you can walk with a baby in your arms, you can dance! So turn up the music and shake your bootie, Mama! Get up out of that chair and move and wiggle and shimmy and twirl and dance like a fool until your heart is pounding and your breath is moving into places it forgot you even had! Dance fast and wild and hot. Dance slow and graceful. Dance in a dignified and elegant manner even though you're dressed in dirty sweats. Dance in your wheelchair, dance the vacuum right into those pesky corners, but just dance! (If you're chaperoning the school dance, keep it small and quiet or your teenager will never speak to you again.) Dance in the kitchen, the hallway, the backyard, and don't be too shy to jig a little in the checkout line. Do the hokey-pokey and turn yourself around. That's what it's all about!

Dare

Dare to do it differently! Dare to be the first mother to boycott standardized testing. Dare to be the last to give your okay to ear piercing. Dare to just say no to circumcision. (Double dare if you're Jewish!) Dare to say yes to nursing your three-year-old, no matter what anyone else says. Read all you can, ponder your decision long and hard, then dare to question the safety of childhood immunizations. When your mother recites her Ten Commandments of Child Discipline, dare to hug her and say, "Thanks, Mom, but I'd like to try out my own ideas." Dare to look and feel and act ten years younger than your age. Dare to ask your grandfather to step outside with his cigar. Dare to tell the truth to first-time mothers and dare them to ignore you and rely on their own experience. Dare to create a model of mothering that you've never seen or heard of before. Then dare to ignore anybody who questions the rightness of that model for you.

Dates

Dinner and an R-rated movie with Dad. Pizza
and beer with the women you met on the subway.
Skiing with Sue followed by nightcaps with
Donna. Shopping for school clothes, just the two
of you. Rockhounding with Nana and Pop-Pop,
then ice cream. A lecture on Buddhism with your
old high-school flame. An African dance class
with your nephew from Sweden. Alone in the
library, talking to no one. A walk by the river and
moonlight above. Brunch with your firstborn—
and for the first time, he's paying. New Year's Eve
in a cabin without a phone. Dancing till dawn
and sunrise by the bay. Mother's Day supper and
an armload of roses. Bowling. Swimming. Rodeo
and square dancing at the fairgrounds. A facial
and a makeover and gallery-hopping with your
very best friend. Off the road in the desert. Top
of the city in L.A. Under the willow tree,
picnicking on smoked trout and capers. It feels so
special. It must be a date!

Dawn

If you've been up all night, why not pause and greet the dawn? There's nothing quite like first light to give you a humbling perspective on the day that's about to begin. The slate was wiped clean in the night, a fresh palette chosen, and all is newly born. State your intention for this dawning day. Will you make it productive? Restful? A day set aside for recharging tired batteries, or for rocketing into high-voltage activity? Declare the keynote for this awakening time and space. Is it greater patience? Firmer boundaries? A new appreciation for the trials and tribulations of a thirteen-year-old? Morning is breaking all around you, cracking open bright possibilities in each glowing band of orange-red. Whatever yesterday offered has fallen away, as you stand facing today. Farewell to the darkness, now welcome the light. This dawn is birthing itself into day.

Deal

Sometimes life deals you a difficult hand. You can't reshuffle. You just play your cards the best you can. You were hoping for four aces and a pair of twos showed up instead. You were counting on the new job and it fell through. You thought the baby just had a cold, but he took a turn for the worse. You sought support but it wasn't there. Just deal. Take stock of the situation and take baby steps in whichever direction you are able. Just deal with what's in front of you right now. Focus. Make the one phone call you need to make. Talk to the one person you're avoiding most. Accept the reality that lies two inches in front of your face. Work with what you have while at the same time you're creating something better. You may feel yourself battered by tsunami waves from all directions. Everything you hold dear may disappear before your very eyes. Surrender to fate. Just deal.

Delegate

If you ever want to get finished, divvy up the work. Assign the oldest to do the dishes; the youngest to sweep the floor. Give the kitty litter cleanup job to the one who leaves the biggest mess in the bathroom—and hope he'll take the hint. Ask for volunteers to sort the recyclables and if no one steps forward, delegate the job to whoever drinks the most soda. Send the newest licensed driver on the coveted assignment to pick up milk and bread. You're far too qualified to scrub the bathtub, so delegate it to someone else. You're tired after work, so someone else can walk the dog. Clean out the gutters? Delegate to whoever likes ladders. Wash the car? Delegate to someone who lives for the opportunity to parade around in a bathing suit top. Anyone can shovel the walk free of snow. The only job you can't delegate is yours.

Delight

Take delight in all of your senses! See the delight in your child's eyes when you show him a picture of Daddy. Smell the delightful aroma of **roses cut fresh** and still misted with dew. Feel yourself fill with a pleasurable glow at the delightful touch of your lover's hands. When you hear the news, be delighted. Be delighted to be who you are. Revel in tiny, delicious delights. Savor the taste of a **cherry-filled chocolate**. Revel in the richness of a warm chenille throw. Do you know the delight of a wet springtime snow? Have you swooned at the sight of a full harvest moon? Spend an evening under the stars while delightful music fills the air. Bask in the warmth of the late morning sun. Delight can be yours if you know where to find it. **Everywhere you look, discover delight.**

Demons

Everybody's got some. Yours will show up at the
least opportune moment. Especially when you're
raw and fragile and exhausted to the bone. They'll
leap up in your face and blow smoke and flames,
and do everything they can to throw you off
center. Your head will fill with old, useless tapes of
self-criticism, judgment, or fear. You'll feel overcome with a sense of helplessness, scarcity, or lack
of self-worth. Demons are a bit like children.
They'll try anything to get your attention, and the
more you ignore them, the more infuriated they
become. Acknowledge them and take a few
moments to listen to their vile and toxic spewings.
Thank them for their input. Firmly yet gently
explain that they have no hold on you. Then send
them on their demon ways. Eventually, they'll get
bored with your lack of reaction. Then you can
look forward to demon-free days.

Details

One eats wheat but no dairy and the other does eggs but never peanuts. If you accidentally put strawberries in the salad, your sister will get diarrhea and your brother is sure to get hives. You always, always leave the key on the hook under the counter (even though you always find it on the frame of the door). The clock on the stove is twelve minutes late and the computer always reads seventeen minutes early. Your youngest is the one whose birth certificate got lost—or is it her brother? You have the same password for every account, except the one where the three comes after the nine. After-school care ends promptly at 6:30 every day, except when they extend it until 7:00. If you're late, you pay an extra ten dollars, unless you notify by 4:23. The van needs a minimum of 87 octane and the station on the east side of town is always three cents cheaper per gallon. A greater truth there never was: Life is in the details.

Detour

Somewhere along the way to painting the kitchen floor, you end up entering art school. The floor still needs painting, but you're on a different journey. You're making great strides toward finishing your screenplay, and right before the climax, you end up buying a house. The movie's never finished, but you really don't care. You agree to coordinate the school graduation, and at the very first meeting, decide you've waited long enough to get your teaching certificate. Someone else orders the programs, and you're traveling a different road. Detours have a way of taking us down pathways we might never have noticed. You stopped at a roadside store to use the bathroom, and before you even got there, the owner offered you a job. You were just going for your checkup, and as soon as you opened your mouth, you fell in love with the dental hygienist. You've got a new relationship and your teeth are looking fab!

Dig

Below the surface lies a rich mother lode. The vein is bursting with gems of wisdom and brilliant pockets of self-knowledge—and the only way to get there is dig. The tools for this digging are many. You can dig into your past, relying on dreams and memories as your sharpest tools. You can take your digging into the garden, where every root and stone that you dig from below is a symbol for something about you. The farther and faster you dig, the more muck and mud and decay will rise up around you. Just as you make progress with digging, it will all begin to feel hopeless. You may grow tired of the digging, ready to throw your trowel in the bottom of the deepest hole, and nevermore enter the mine. Take heart! Keep on digging! You'll unearth your treasures. And once you strike gold, you'll start digging again.

Distance

One of life's great paradoxes is how distance can help bring things closer together. It goes beyond the adage that absence makes the heart grow fonder. When you're standing in the middle of a fast-running stream, it can feel like a torrential river. Everything is magnified; every twist and turn seems terrifying. By stepping back onto shore and putting distance between you, the perspective is altogether different and the threat not nearly so large. When your family is embroiled in the midst of conflict, it may seem large enough to swallow everyone up. Step away from the center of the storm and watch it lose its power. Give it some space; give it some distance. Boulders will turn into pebbles. Problems won't loom overhead. Keep your distance and watch how easily it all will come together.

Diva

You're the queen! You're the empress! You're the mom! No kitchen celebrity packs them in for three shows each day quite like you do. You're the leading lady of the living room and every day you put in an Oscar-winning performance. Your fans chase you morning and night. You can barely escape to the bathroom. Your rendition of Goldilocks has them on the edge of their chairs. Your singing brings them to their feet in thunderous applause. Do your famous imitation of Dad and they're rolling in the aisles. Every dinner is a command performance. Your pancakes are smashing! Brava! Take a bow! You'd never trade this role for fame or for fortune. You're the diva. You're the star. You're the tops. Move over starlets, the diva's in town. Who says so? Says you! You the mom!

Do

Do what you can for your children, but don't do it all. Let them learn to do for themselves. Do her hair until she can do it herself. Do his boots until he's got the knack. Help with their homework, but remember it's not yours to do. The more you do for others, the less they learn to do. Get everyone involved in doing the dishes as soon as it's safe. Give lessons in doing the laundry as early as you can. Do your best and know that it is enough. Who ever said you have to do everything? Who ever told you it had to be perfect? Do it your way, in your time, at your pace. Or choose not to do it at all. Do what you love. Do what makes your heart sing. Do what serves the greater good and know that it's best for you, too. As you do for others, let others do for you. You're doing no one any favors when you try to do it all.

Doze

A mom's gotta get it where she can. Catnaps in the car, twenty winks while waiting at the Y, and a pre-dinner doze in the driveway. All around you, moms are doing the doze. They're hiding their eyes behind hats, cradling their heads on coffee shop counters, and sawing logs while waiting with feet in the stirrups. Drifting off during dance class, lightly snoring at the senior class play. Heads back and mouths wide open in the last row at the gymkhana meet. Give a mom ten minutes and she'll take a nap. Offer her a chair and she's off to a heavenly dreamland. Give her a facial and she'll doze for an hour under a bright, blinding lamp. Shampoo her hair and put her under the dryer and oops, within minutes, she's gone! Unless someone's bleeding or there's flood or there's fire, don't disturb a mom when she's doing her doze.

Drama

If you need some drama in your life, go to the theater. Take in a matinee. It's a great deal more enjoyable than creating the kind of trauma drama that turns family life into a Shakespearean epic. Heart-stopping tragedy, deception, and betrayal make for great entertainment, but they're hard to tackle off stage. Comic buffoonery is great for laughs, but it loses something when translated to the living room stage. Weeping and wailing and gnashing of teeth can keep an audience enthralled, but it's a little bit much to handle at breakfast. Is it possible to cut down on the household histrionics? Must everything be so dramatic? If your heart's desire is to be a drama queen, consider the community playhouse. At home, try to keep the white-knuckle thrills to a reasonable level, and let the curtain fall on oh-so-much drama.

Dreams

I dreamed I was in a beautiful castle and my every need was satisfied. Just by thinking, it was so. I dreamed I could fly by closing my eyes and imagining myself a beautiful silver bird. I dreamed the new addition was finished and it cost less than we expected. I dreamed my daughter had one good friend she could call her own. I dreamed the house stayed clean for a full twenty-four hours. Then I dreamed it happened again. I dreamed my new tortilla shop turned a profit in just six months, and my banker turned into a unicorn and galloped off into the sunset. I dreamed every child on earth had a loving home and good food, and a life filled with laughter and joy. I held on to my dreams and nurtured my wishes, and then, just like that, they came true.

Drop

Okay, drop it. Drop the mask you've been
wearing so long that you wouldn't recognize yourself if you met face-to-face in the desert. Drop
the act. Drop the illusion that you are living
somebody else's life instead of your own. Let your
voice drop down into your belly and start
speaking in your authentic tone and timbre. First,
drop the kids off at the teen center. Then drop
the shirts at the laundry. And don't forget to drop
everything and rush home to meet the lawn-
mower guy. Drop that false edge—it doesn't
become you. Drop the pretense and just be who
you are. That accent you've been working so hard
to cultivate? Drop it. But first, drop a hundred
bucks at the grocery and come home with
nothing to eat. Then drop by to check on Mom's
azaleas. Pull into the driveway just as a water
balloon drops from the roof above you.
Then cruise into
            the house without
                        dropping a beat.

86

Earth

There are days a mother can fly apart at the seams, and she needs to get back down to earth. She needs to feel solid ground under her feet and walk on soil, sand, or stone. She needs to imagine her roots going deep into the earth and up through her legs and steadying her stance. That's when a mother needs to reconnect with the soil. To dig deep and stir up old leaves and twigs and bugs from below. Mother Earth has a heartbeat all her own, and its rhythm can be felt by all mothers. Find it in the garden, the playground, the park, or the beach. It will call to you from grassland and mountain, riverbank and marsh, meadow and forest. When the roads and the buildings are closing around you, there's nothing more grounding than sweet Mother Earth.

Embody

Bring your experience out of the ethers and into your body. Stop thinking and talking about change and move into meaningful action. If you're ready to stretch your professional boundaries, start with a dance class with plenty of stretching. If you're feeling a need to create space from your child, take off your sling and start using a stroller. When it's grounding you need, dig in the earth. Rake, shovel, plant, walk in the woods, or lie down in the grass and embody the grounding you seek. Before you teach anything, live it. Before you write a word, make it real. If you're seeking to clear inner clutter, start with your closets. If you want to slow down your pace, take a slow, peaceful walk. When you're itching to move, rearrange the furniture. When you're craving more freedom, take off your bra. Once you feel it in your body, you can embrace what you want and know that it's yours.

Endings

An ending is nothing more than preparation for a new beginning. When your little one stops nursing, you both step up to new levels of independence. When that long-lived love affair with blankie is over, she's ready to embrace a new kind of best friend. Your maternity leave might be ending, but you're beginning a new life as a working mother. The day will come when you and your son can no longer fit together on the rocking chair—and that's the day you get a new sofa! Every relationship that falls by the wayside opens a door for someone new to walk through. Every game that gets called on account of rain moves you toward a fresh start of 0–0 (instead of continuing at 26–2). Just like every cloud has its silver lining, every end portends a beginning right around the bend.

Endless

Endless laundry, endless love. Endless kisses, forever hugs. No end to the stains that appear on the rug. The whole thing's never-ending! Endless bliss and endless pain. When you're craving the sunshine, you get endless rain! Five pounds more? Must be water-weight gain. Is any of this ever ending? Look at these diapers! They never end. Who chewed the contract I was preparing to send? A lifetime of family, a lifetime of friends. Looks like it never will end. Endless piles of endless stuff. Endless days when everything feels rough. When does this phase end, Mister Tough? May all of this go on forever.

Endure

Stay on track, no matter what. Make your way
through dark nights of the soul and slither
through your shadows and know there's a rainbow
at the end of the road. Stand firm in your truth
while others wobble. Outlast whoever believes the
last word is hers. Do without, then do without
more if you must. Hold space for the vision
you've carried so long, and know you can hold it
some more. There will be a last diaper to change,
and until it appears, just keep at it. Your child will
learn to pick up his clothes, and the wait till he
does will be worth it. You never are given more
than you can handle. No matter the journey,
you'll make it in time. Whatever's dished out, you
can take it. Is there really so much that you're
asked to endure?

Energy

It's not just how much is in your tank, but the
quality of the fuel. Frenetic, go-go, get-the-job-
done energy might give you a quick start, but it
will leave you in the long run. Victim energy
might garner sympathy and declare you a martyr,
but soon everyone will feel drained without
knowing why. If you're running on fumes, you'll
never make it. If you're running on resentment,
you'll make it miserable. If anger feeds your fire,
you're going to run yourself into the ground. Let
pure, clean-burning energy flow through you
from a source that never dries up. See yourself as
a conduit, not a power plant—and the well will
never be empty. Let energy move through you,
not from you, and your ultimate source can
power the world. If you feel you're running on
empty most of the time, fill up at a new kind of
station. Know that you are the pipeline and not
the supply.

Enough

Enough already! Enough arguing and complaining and definitely, enough smart-mouthed backtalk. **Enough is enough.** How many pairs of jeans do you need? You already have enough. How many CDs have you bought this week? It seems like more than enough. How many times have you driven to the arcade? Enough is enough is enough. You've gone way overboard this time; you should have stopped when you got to enough. How many times will you let them disrespect you? Even one time is too much. How many times do you have to be told? **Actually, once is enough.** How much longer can all this continue? Enough is enough is enough. Enough already of this conversation. You've had more than enough to last all year long. You've listened enough to thoroughly convince you: Enough is enough is enough is enough.

Escape

Get away from it all when you can. For an hour, for a day, for a weekend. Escape from all the little voices and arms and needs that pull at you every day from every direction. See that everyone is safe and cared for, then make your getaway as if your life depends on it. Because it does. Escape through the door, down the highway, into the garden, out to the woods, up to the rooftop, around the corner or over the border or above the clouds. Escape into a film where the lovers ride off into the sunset. Get lost in the lilting melody of old Celtic ballads. Dive into a book where escape eludes the heroine until at last she steps into a forest where the only sound she hears is her own beating heart. Step into the rare hush of an old country church or a cathedral in the center of town. In the recesses of your mind, create a picture of your perfect escape. To keep it alive, visit often.

Essentials

Air. Water. Food. Love. Ponder what is truly
essential. How much can you strip away and
never miss at all? Home. Work. Truth. Love. Out
of all that you own, how much is simply window
dressing? If your life depended on having less,
what would you want most to possess? Authenticity. Communication. Relationships. Love. In
the rush to have everything, it's worth your time
to reflect on what is enough. On what is essential.
On what you and your loved ones truly need.
Peace. Joy. Family. Love. Respect. Trust. Purpose.
Some essentials are universal and others very, very
personal. Painting. Dance. Writing. Song. Earth.
Sky. Spirit. Prayer. When you get too far beyond
what you require, everything takes on less impor-
tance. Money. Cars. Clothes. Status. Position.
Power. Control. Only you discern what is
essential.

Excuse

Excuse yourself. Get up from the table and leave the room when the conversation makes you uncomfortable. Excuse yourself from the meeting when hidden agendas are taking control. Refuse to waste your time listening to boring, self-absorbed monologues by people you barely know. Don't say you have another appointment. Don't feign a phone call. Don't pretend that your car is being towed. Just excuse yourself. When someone presses you for answers to personal questions, say, "Excuse me, I don't think that's really your business." Thank your child for sharing the news that burping is a compliment in some foreign countries—and remind her that "Excuse me" is still the norm here at home. Tell your sixteen-year-old that when the evening takes a dangerous direction, it's okay to excuse himself without a single word. Don't make up excuses when you need to be excused. Let your lips mouth the words, "Excuse me."

Exercise

A sly mom will tell you she never need exercise, 'cause her kids keep her running all day. Nice try. Not even the most energetic toddler will get your heart and lungs pumping enough to wake up every blood cell in your body. No matter how many toys you pick up off the floor, it's not going to tone up that bottom. You will not sculpt definition in your arms just from folding the laundry. Find the reason that's going to get you working out. It can be that you want to live a little longer to enjoy your kids. It might be that you want to spend all summer on the beach in a bikini. Maybe you're tired of losing time and again when everybody races up the stairs. Or maybe you're just plain tired. Get up and get out and get moving that body! You're not getting another, so start exercising today!

Expand

Push out your edges and be as big as you want to
be. Expand your horizons beyond what you imagined you could ever allow. Travel farther than
anyone in your family and take in experiences
richer than you thought you could handle.
Expand your views. Read the stories of mothers
who raised their children during the Great
Depression. Listen to mothers beg for food for
their children and life for their sons. Expand your
compassion even as your gratitude grows. Take on
a larger worldview and a deeper understanding of
your own inner life. Expand your capacity to walk
in the shoes of another and to feel the blisters and
calluses they feel. Take your trust up another
notch. Carry yourself to a higher level. Create a
container big enough to hold the people you care
for. Expand from the heart and watch how you
grow.

Experience

Ultimately, all you have is your own experience. You can read about others' experiences, watch them move past you on the big screen, and observe them up close and personal. But all you'll ever truly know, like you know the back of your hand, is what you experience. Not what you think about in your mind, but what you feel in your body. What does it matter what the experts say, if you experience something altogether different? How can you subscribe to conventional wisdom—when your own body's wisdom cries out a different tune? If you think you're supposed to be joyful, yet you feel a huge hole in the pit of your being, what will you believe? If the mothering experience is portrayed as light pink, and your days and nights feel dark red, which is the truth that is yours? All you can rely upon is your own experience, and trust that others will rely on theirs.

Expose

Expose a little more so people get a glimpse of who you really are. Let them see what lies beneath the surface. Expose that soft, sweet underbelly that lives below your cool unflappable exterior. Have the courage to speak about your deep relationship with your God and your undeniable commitment to your faith. There are skeletons in closets that must be exposed. There are dark secrets buried under years of lies and deceptions, and they must be uncovered. Expose your children to more and more truth as they are ready. Tear down that wallboard in the kitchen and expose the antique bricks underneath. Rip up the old linoleum and who knows what treasures might be exposed? Like a camera, long, slow exposures make best use of your light. Be willing to uncover a bit at a time, so you don't need to feel too exposed.

Faces

Oh, the faces you'll meet! Cherubic faces with angel-kissed lips, ringed by a golden-soft halo of curls. Faces that could stop a clock. Round chubby faces. Long, drawn faces. Faces that remind you of your great-aunt Sadie when she had just finished up with her prayers. Heaven lives in the face of a newborn. Clouds take up residence behind dark, pouty eyes. "Don't give me that look, young lady!" Teary faces. Smeary faces. Sunny, funny, cheery faces. Kids can read your face like a book. You may think you're hiding behind glisteny eyes, but they always know if you've been crying. You can try to maintain a quiet veneer, but a twitch in your cheek says you're bursting to tell all! Face facts! You can practice your bluffing for hours. You can amaze your friends with your poker visage, but you'll never keep secrets from any of your children. They always know what's happening behind Mommy's eyes.

Faith

Travel beyond reason to faith. Believe in the baby that has not yet arrived, and have faith that he will when it's time. Have faith that there's a house with a garden waiting for you, even if you haven't yet seen it. Rely on faith when you just can't bring yourself to believe the numbers and promises that they keep throwing your way. Have faith that love will carry you through this rocky stretch, though you don't have a clue how it will happen.

Continue to trust your own intuition even when all around you, others are turning from theirs. Have faith that your teenager's momentary misdirection will correct itself, and have faith that higher wisdom will prevail. After you lay down your need to understand and figure out and predict every outcome, carry faith in your heart that all happens for a reason. And keep the faith that it's not yours to know.

Fall

Feel yourself slipping? Just fall. Fall into the waiting arms of someone who's been waiting for you to fall. Fall to your knees and ask for help. Fall into bed after sitting up all night with a frightened and croupy child. Fall asleep with all your clothes on and immediately fall into a deep state of dreaming. Watch the snow fall for hours and fall into giggles thinking how you always fall down on your skis. Fall apart a little. Fall apart a lot. Find a shoulder to lean on and fall against it. Get a running start, jump higher than the sky and then fall into a pile of autumn leaves with your baby in your arms. Once in a while, take your hair down and let it fall softly on your shoulders. Try not to notice how much has fallen out. If you fall behind, know you'll catch up. You'll pick things up after the fall.

Family

There's family you were born into and there's family you choose. Family that shares a stormy past and family who is creating a blissful future. Who do you call family? The blood relation you haven't spoken with in over twenty-two years—or the neighbor who brings your mail to your door every day? Is blood thicker than the water of spiritual connection—or is it just a different vintage? Expand your vision of family to include the grandmother who helps your child cross the street before and after school. The birds who have nested in the eaves of your attic. The shopkeepers who knead the bread you eat and blend your breakfast smoothie. The rivers and streams you drive by each morning. See yourself as one link in a vast global family. Know that the world is home to all your relations. In all things, do your best to keep your family from harm.

Fathers

Where there's a mother, there's a father. He may be present or absent, engaged or distant, bonded or estranged. He may sit up all night with a feverish child or send a check every month without fail. He's your very best friend and life-long companion, your former, your ex-, or your never-quite-was. By birth or by choice, he's a father. Fathers do nearly everything mothers do. They give bedtime baths and tell bedtime stories and trim little toenails and kiss little toes. Dads braid hair and take the stains out of jeans and hold hands on the way to the dentist. They're lovers, providers, supporters, and friends—there at the beginning and there at the end. There for the blood and there for the tears; for the trials and triumphs, the hopes and the fears. Sing praise for the fathers who carry their share. The poppas, the daddies, *los padres*, *les pères*.

Favorites

Your very favorite time of day: sunrise. Your very favorite place: home. Your favorite meal: someone else's chicken cacciatore. Your favorite tourist destination: San Francisco. Your favorite coffee shop is the one on the pedestrian mall where you can people-watch for hours. The one that makes your very favorite banana cream pie. Favorite poet? Emily Dickinson. All-time favorite movie? *Shakespeare in Love.* Your favorite New Year's Eve was the one you ushered in with a new daughter. Favorite cookie: oatmeal walnut. Favorite music: mellow jazz. Favorite surprise: long-stemmed roses sent with a message from overseas. Favorite fantasy: three weeks on a deserted island with your real-life lover and not much else. You'll never have any favorite where your children are concerned. That's one place there's no room for favorites.

Feel

Stop thinking so much and start feeling so much more! Bring that elevator of thoughts and feelings down from the top floor and feel your emotions in your belly where they belong. Every time you try to hide your feelings, a part of yourself is lost. Feel the red hot heat of anger when it flares up, and find a safe way to channel it. Feel the pink flush of love radiating to your fingertips when you gaze at your sleeping angel baby. Feel how it feels to speak your truth, like butterflies and lions dancing together inside you. Feel how contentment feels—white and pure and still. Pound the ground in frustration. Sing out with joy. Undulate to an African drumbeat. Feeling is a gift that keeps on giving: your children come to know their feelings when you show honestly how feelings feel.

Fill

Think of your mothering life as a big beautiful bowl, and fill it with things that bring you joy. Health. Balance. Music. Dance. Walks on cool green grass or hot white sand or smooth wood floors. Fill your bowl with flowers and an extravagant dessert now and then, with time away from the computer and close to those you love. When your bowl is filled to the brim, empty it out and fill it again. With a history class at the local college, a cooking class at the community center, long hours reading philosophy or theology or travelogues from the nineteenth century. Fill your bowl with friends who will be there when you call. With dreams and the power to make them come true. Fill your home with color, with textures, with luscious smells and tastes and tiny things that you've picked up along the way. And when your bowl is filled to the brim, empty it out so you can fill it again.

Find

Do you ever find yourself asking huge, unanswerable questions? Do you wonder how a hummingbird can find its way across a continent? Do you question whether there's any hope to be found in unspeakable tragedy? Have you spent endless hours pondering whether anyone will ever find the lid to the Crock-Pot? You won't find if you never seek. If you're feeling a bit lost inside, find your way home. Click your heels three times and you'll find you never really left. Find at least one woman who can help you find your way. Find fellowship with others, and find direction that will help you find sustenance for your soul. Find something every day to talk about with your children. Find their dirty socks under the seat cushion and find that note from the teacher six weeks too late. If you can't find your car keys, find a reason to stay.

Fingers

You'll never find a better tool than what you've got in fingers. Mothers do more finger things in a day than most people do in a week. Mothers' fingers tie and untie, and snap and unsnap, and braid pigtails and twirl curly ribbon and get zippers started that no one else can. They train their fingers to do intricate tricks like clasping necklaces behind their backs in the dark and miraculously finding the start of the tape. Fingers dig peas out of all kinds of places, play concertos for flute and piano, and flawlessly perform "Here Comes Thumbkin" almost whenever requested. Mothers' fingers give babies something to grasp on, to teeth on, and to suck on when nothing better is available. In a pinch, fingers fill in for forks, spoons, and claw hammers, and for licking the frosting bowl clean. Let's not forget mothers' fingers: these dexterous digits lead straight to mothers' hearts.

Finish

You can barely finish a sentence without interruption, but the quarterly reports will be finished tomorrow if it takes you all night. Your new home office is nearly finished. As soon as you stitch up the curtains, you're done. After four long years, you're finished with college. No more assignments, no more exams. "Who finished up my favorite shampoo?" "Who ate the rest of my fine Stilton cheese?" That pesky mouse that's been chewing on crackers met up with the cat and he's finished for good! When it comes to the dishes, you never are finished. You do mountains of laundry and still you're not done. There's never enough time to read the Sunday paper. But with all of those sections, can't you at least finish one? You restart your thoughts thirty times every day. For once can they just let you finish?

Fire

There's a fire burning inside you, whether it's been damped down to a single glowing ember, or it's threatening to rage out of control. Either way, you'd best not play with fire or someone's bound to get burned. You can fan the flames of your inner fire gently, with inspiring art, music, or conversation. You can toss a few logs on your fire by striking out in a new direction, by hooking up with equally passionate people, or by keeping your distance from those who want desperately to douse your dreams. When you've got a good fire going in your belly, keep it in the fireplace where you can put it to good use. Direct your heat and passion into safe outlets where you can cook up something warm and nourishing. When you start tossing your fire around like a fire-breathing dragon, you don't need a fire extinguisher. All you need is to channel your fire.

Fit

You can try on a closetful of clothes labeled "mother" only to find that few of them fit. This one's too smothery, yards and yards of fabric that can wrap around a child until he all but disappears. The other is too light and breezy, wafting in the wind and never quite sufficient to shelter from the cold. Here's something in well-worn, baby-soft flannel. Perfect for cuddling and snuggling for hours on end; but unable to take a crease and hold an edge when needed. What truly fits you as a mother? Wrinkled and casual, ready to get down on the floor and play whenever the impulse arises? Starched and formal, keeping your proper distance between parent and child and holding yourself close to the vest? You'll know when you've found a mothering style that's your perfect fit. It will fit you like a glove, last a lifetime, and feel so comfortable that you'll never want to change.

Flee

If you must, flee. For the safety of yourself and
your children, get out of harm's way as fast as you
can. Flee from any situation that has the potential
to explode into danger. Flee from any individual
who threatens you or anyone in your care. You
don't need anyone's permission to flee. There are
times when it's good to stay and work things out.
There are times when you're ready to flee. To fly.
To remove yourself from toxic surroundings that
will never support your well-being. Listen to your
own intuition and you'll know that your only
choice is to flee. Confide in one or two friends
who will honor your decision, and they will help
you flee. Flee to a safe haven, to a secret refuge.
Take the children and flee. Pack your courage,
your strength and trust all will be well. You don't
need much else when you flee.

Flexibility

There's no crash course in flexibility more
powerful than children in the house. So give in
early and kiss your schedules, your rules, and your
organizational management theories goodbye! The
minute you believe you've got it under control,
one sly two-year-old can move in and bring you
to your knees in no time. Cast anything at all in
stone, and within moments, it will be smashed to
smithereens. If you ever said *never* before—you'll
never say it again. Bending and stretching with
your newfound flexibility might drive others
crazy, but it will leave you more limber than a
yogi. You'll show up at the dentist when naptime
is over. Make your lunchtime appointment sometime before three. And get yourself into the
shower, oh, well, whenever. It's not so tough to
choose between being a control freak and being a
mother. One might get you a blue ribbon rating
for efficiency, but the other is a lot more fun.

Flow

Let yourself be carried along by the flow. Relax and go where the energy is going, instead of exhausting yourself trying to fight it. If you're determined to get something done and everything imaginable gets in your way, drop the idea or save it for another day. When you want a swim date and everyone else is shouting, "Movie!" go with the flow. Why pick this night to make your eight-course Hunan dinner, when the consensus is that waffles will do just fine? Sometimes it's so easy to give in and just go along for the ride. Watch how a leaf is effortlessly carried down a stream. Ever see a shell fight its way out when the tide is obviously moving in? Let go of your flow. Unless you're a salmon, swimming upstream is never worth the battle.

Flowers

Never underestimate the power of a flower. Inside a single bloom is a symphony to lift your spirits and soothe your soul. Invite a vase of daisies into your kitchen and dinnertime takes on a bright new glow. Sprinkle rose petals across a shelf and who knows what will happen next? Flowers bring autumn into your home and spring into your heart and fill the air with summer all year round. They remind us how fragile life really is, that what is beautiful and blooming and bursting with life today, can lose its luster in the blink of an eye. Whenever you're able, surround yourself with flowers. Don't wait for someone to send them: buy flowers yourself, or better still, grow your own.

Focus

You can multitask like a master, but what does it matter? The more you do, the less chance you'll do anything well. Clear the decks and focus on one thing at a time. Is it really vital that you mix up a potato salad while faxing a report to Thailand and watching TV? Contain your energy rather than scattering it in twelve directions. Ever see a child watch the action on an anthill? Every muscle, every pore is focused like a laser on that one miniature landscape. She sees detail a mere glance would never reveal. Two ice cream trucks could jingle by and she'd never even notice. You experience so much more when you focus. Look into the eyes of the person you're talking to and really hear his words and notice that little curl right above his cheek. Keep turning this way and that and everything is fuzzy. When you stop spinning around, then you focus.

Follow

Follow your instincts, wherever they lead you. Follow your heart into uncharted waters and trust that love will follow. Let someone else take the lead now and then. Do you feel somehow less when you follow? Is your impulse to pass whoever you follow? Follow the trail of intrigue to discover the truth. Where truth lives, goodness will follow. If you see tracks in the snow, follow them. If you hear the lilting sound of a flute, let your ears follow the tune. Your child may not choose to follow in your footsteps, but leave them anyway so he trusts there's a choice. Follow your feelings with words and follow your words with action. Know that in the dance called life, sometimes you lead and sometimes you follow. Strange it may seem, but sometimes it's the leader who follows.

Forever

Once a mother, always a mother. No matter how old your children are, no matter how seldom you see them, you are forever a mother. You may have lost your child before birth, or during adolescence, or after the age of fifty. Perhaps you had precious little time with a child you had prayed for. You still have a mother's heart that can never be taken away. Mother is not just a box you check on a form. It's not simply a label for those who have birthed from their bellies. There are no prerequisites of time or of space. Mothering is a state of unalterable being. See the commotion when a baby enters a room. Watch the women's eyes light up; see them gather round and coo like doves. For now and forever, a mother's a mother. For at the heart of every mother is limitless love.

Forget

Forget nearly everything they ever taught you.
Choose what you will remember and what you
choose to forget. Forget what they said about
people who look different, talk different, eat
different, live different. Forget their outdated
attitudes about color and status and class. Forget a
good bit of what they told you was right, and
forget even more of what they assured you was
wrong. You know how everybody froze up and
shut down when things got close to the heart?
Forget it ever happened. Forget everything you
learned about disciplining a child with fear, with
shame, with violence. Forge your own beliefs,
your own philosophy, your own way of mothering. Forget those rules about what you can do
with your own life and what you can't. When
they ask, "Don't you remember a thing that we
taught you?" say, "Sorry, I think I forgot!"

Forgiveness

The most important person you'll ever forgive is you. Forgive yourself for not being the perfect mother (whatever that is!). Forgive yourself for being blinded by love (or by fear or by attraction or fill in the blank). Forgive yourself for having children too early, too late, in or out of the right or wrong marriage, or any combination of the above. Wash away guilt with forgiveness. Cleanse yourself of regret through forgiveness. If you can't find a way to forgive yourself for making choices that now seem less than ideal, how can you imagine that others can possibly find their way? How will you move through forgiveness? Write a letter of forgiveness to yourself. Sing a forgiving song. Dance your forgiveness into the floor. Bead a necklace of forgiveness, knit a scarf of forgiveness, and let forgiveness drop out of every finger as you work. Wear your forgiveness close to your heart, where you'll be certain not to forget it.

Freedom

Find your freedom in mothering. Taste the
freedom of leaving the high-pressure work world
for time at home. Feel free enough to play and
discover. To ask questions and seek answers and
grow alongside your child in beautiful ways. In
the company of young ones, a freedom exists that
you won't find in the adult world. Take a deep
breath of this freedom. With every step of independence your children take, take a few steps of
your own. Free up your thinking; liberate old
attitudes and ways of being that keep everyone in
the house from soaring free. Structure isn't a
prison; it's a framework that can support you as
you test out new freedoms. What tools for living
free will you hand to your child? How will you
help him to free up his passion? How will you
show her to live her own truth? Exercise your
right to choose. Flex your muscles of freedom.

Friends

You've got to have friends. Real ones. The kind you can call at 2:35 A.M. to meet you at the emergency room or the police station or the all-night diner. Friends who will feed your cats when you're on vacation. Who will make you peppermint tea and never ever once say "I told you so!" while you pour out your heart and your tears. You've got to have friends. Old friends who know where you've been, and new friends who see where you're going. Friends who had their babies years ago and can share their experience without needing to step on yours. Who can hear you without judgment when you admit there were times you wanted to lay your baby down in a field of flowers and walk away. You simply must have one friend who can help you ask the questions without needing to know the answers. You can have a soul mate and a life partner and a spouse and a mother and sisters and all the children you could ever want. And even then, you've got to have friends.

Frustration

Frustration has its place. It can create sufficient pressure to push you to a point where you know that you won't take it anymore. Managed properly, the energy of frustration can provide high-octane fuel to propel you into healthier new directions. What frustrates you most? If you're frustrated that they don't listen to you, maybe you're not speaking as clearly as you believe. If your frustration comes from a sense of being pulled in every direction, maybe it's a message that you're not attending to your center. When you feel a growing sense of frustration around the heavy burden you think you have to carry, chances are good you're finally ready to lighten up and share the load. Frustration can be the spark that ignites a smoldering fire. Listen to the story your frustration is trying to tell you. Blow a little steam off and you can use frustration well.

Garden

We could always find Mother in her garden. Straw hat cocked to one side and smudges of dirt on her cheeks, and a serenity she found nowhere else. She hummed as she worked on her knees, bringing the dark, moist soil to her face and breathing in its earthy deliciousness. She seemed to bow reverently to each weed before she released it from its home; she planted each seed with a prayer. At times, she paused and peered into the black earth below as though they were sharing a secret. Somehow we knew not to interrupt her reverie. In the garden, Mother always seemed untouchable, transported to a place uninhabited by unruly children and workaday cares. We waited quietly by the house as she completed her ritual. Trimmings in the old gray can, cukes and radishes tucked in top jacket pockets, her arms filled with flowers and joy in her eyes.

Gatherings

Wherever two or more of you are gathered, you'll
find good company and great desserts. Gather
with other moms and share what you know about
private schools and public transportation. Better
yet, gather with non-moms and share anything
and everything that has nothing to do with
raising a child. Connect at parties and picnics,
class reunions and professional dinners, and
discover the strength you can find in numbers.
Call six other women and start a monthly gath-
ering to read Sufi poetry. Gather at the park after
dark and join voices in song. Participate in family
gatherings where no one's related and everyone is
kin. Gather in clusters, in twos, threes, and
groupings of thirty. Gather to create ceremony, to
break bread together and repair old engines
together. Frequently, gather in silence if you wish.
Gather fresh sage in summer, then gather 'round
the fire to make prayer ties in the fall.

Give

Give as much as you want, but don't give it all away. Give the gifts that you alone can give and give yourself the freedom to give in the way that gives you joy. Give unconditionally. Attach no strings and expect nothing in return. Give it time. Give it space. Give the universe an opening to work the miracles you could never create on your own. Give another human being the opportunity to love you. Give yourself enough room to receive it. Let go of your grasp and give in. Just give it up. Give up your need to be right, to be first, to be best, to be perfect. Give up your control and ask others to give up theirs. Give it a go! Give yourself permission to give birth to a powerful new culture of giving. Open your heart and give it all you've got.

Good

Good is what you get when you're willing to
forgo perfection. Your painting is good, though
you're not another Picasso. Your children's grades
are good, though they're not National Merit
Scholars. You make a good apple pie, but you've
tasted plenty that are better. Good is worth
striving for. God is good—and that seems to be
enough for most. Goodness carries none of the
pressure that comes with achieving perfection,
and nearly all the rewards. You're a good mother.
A good role model for your children. A good
citizen and a good human being. You're blessed
with good looks and a good heart, and once in a
while, a wee bit of good luck. It's been said that
good is the enemy of perfect. Some enemies are
good to have on your side. Everyone likes the
movie that has a good ending. May all your
beginnings and endings be good.

Grandchildren

Guess who's a grandmother? As far as you're concerned the math just won't add up, but here you are and you're tickled pink and blue. Now you can be the good guy. Now you can play and snuggle and love as long as you want, and then you get to go home. Long-term decisions are not your business. Day-to-day drudgery? It's not your thing. You're the one who can spend all day at the aquarium and spend as much as you want on everything that Mom and Dad never would buy. You can shamelessly brag endlessly about grades and girlfriends and good looks, and no one expects you to blush. Grandchildren keep you young and active and up-to-date on the latest must-have toys and TV. They scarf up your cooking and adore your attention and tell you family secrets at the drop of a hat. It's been said love is better the second time around and so you've been blessed with grandchildren.

Grandeur

Pick yourself up out of your tiny existence and surround yourself with a glimmer of grandeur. Pack up the family and head to a place where the landscape is grander by far than anything ever dreamed up by humans. Drink in mountains and oceans on a grand and glorious scale. Visit a planetarium and insert yourself into the grandeur of the infinite universe. What electric light show could outshine a curtain of stars? Hike through slick-rock canyons shaped by millions of years of wind and water and take pause and ponder the grandeur. Taste the awe of an unbroken horizon that travels forever. The sweep of a valley that moose call home. There are wonders in the world that defy definition. Steep yourself in their glory and you'll know what grandeur means.

Grandparents

Whatever their age, they're a godsend. Grandparents give your child exactly what you cannot. They sit for hours and play when you're hopelessly busy. Go for walks and never rush. Give plenty of tough love when you're feeling weak and bitter. Grandparents love to cook homemade meals that you never learned to master. They sit in rocking chairs and never get bored, and sit with sleeping children on their laps and never get cramps. Grandparents stay calm because they've seen it all before. They don't ask the teenagers too many questions, because they already know most of the answers. They fold the underwear and T-shirts because they know how good it feels to find them that way. Whether Grandpa and Grammy are across town or across the globe, you can be sure that their valentines will arrive on time and their birthday wishes will never be late. On a scale of one to ten, they usually score a thousand. It's no wonder their first name is *grand*!

Gratitude

Gratitude is several steps beyond remembering to say "Thank you." More than just a way of being polite, it's a way of moving through your life. The best way to express your gratitude is to live it every day. Every moment if you can. Begin the day with gratitude. End the day with gratitude. Be grateful for the challenges that are laid in your path as well as the ease and joy. Remember the old saw about the man who pitied himself for having no shoes, until he met a man who had no feet. Be grateful for the shoes and the feet and the legs and the ability to move them. If you don't have it all, be grateful for whatever you do have. Speak your gratitude out loud or silently. "I am grateful for this rainy day, for it fills our lakes and reservoirs." "I am grateful for the speeding ticket, for it reminds me that I am racing through life at a dangerous speed." "I am grateful that my son is too sick to go to school, for it shows me what a gift it is to stay home with him." Gratitude is not after the fact. Live a life of gratitude first—and then be grateful for everything that follows.

Grow

Your child isn't the only one who's growing. Every day, grow a little more into the life that carries your name. Grow into greater ease with your authentic self. Grow wiser and more beautiful with each passing day. Move beyond people and situations you've outgrown, that stifle your budding and blossoming. Grow out of your old, tired stories and step out of the skin that no longer fits. Grow in stature. Rise up to your full height and grow into your grandest vision. Stop playing small! Expand your self-knowledge and embrace a greater truth. Grow intellectually. Grow creatively. Grow herbs for health and bamboo for good fortune. Stretch enough to leap over your own boundaries and discover how large your container can be. Deepen your commitment to your own unfolding. Look in the mirror.

My, how you've grown!

Guarantees

There are none. Period. You can feed your child the highest-quality organic fruits and vegetables, yet there's still no guarantee she won't catch the flu bug that goes around every winter. You can install every child safety device ever made, and accidents will still happen. Guaranteed. A child can be raised on an endless flow of unconditional love and encouragement—and no one can guarantee that he won't still hit some bumpy spots in the highway. A child who grows up in a house filled with books may decide she'd rather watch videos and surf the Internet than read the greatest classics ever written. You can live your entire life for your child, sacrificing your own needs and dreams and pouring every ounce of energy you have directly into your child's well-being. Believing yourself to be the perfect mother, you can end up angry, frustrated, and resentful at your child. And that one's guaranteed.

Guts

She walked away from a beautiful house and a
comfortable living, but she took her self-respect
with her. That woman's got guts! She's got two
kids in school and a third one in diapers, and she
picked up and moved them all to a ranch in
Montana. She applied for a partnership in the
practice three weeks after her husband died—and
that takes some kind of guts. She pulled her
youngest out of school because she didn't like the
teacher's attitude—and you can bet that required
some guts! A mother can call up nerves of steel
when her family's well-being is at stake. She'll
march right into the plant manager's office in the
middle of a meeting and demand straight answers
about pollution. She'll send four pounds of
manure to her legislator to let him know what she
thinks of his politics. Assertiveness works and
chutzpah is stronger—and sometimes you need
plain old guts!

Haircut

Sometimes it can make all the difference in the world. An inch or two here, a quick bang trim, or maybe that giant leap that opens up your face and shows off your eyes and reminds people that you have a neck like a swan. When the day seems like it's going to the dogs, you can turn everything around with a spontaneous trip to the salon. If they can't fit you in for weeks, find somebody who can. Ask a friend to cut your hair, or if you're really brave, ask a child whom you trust with sharp scissors. Get rid of the dead ends and the uneven edges and every single strand that leaves you feeling like yesterday's news. Add some color; add some shine. Do it even if no one older than nine will notice. Do it even if you did it last week and you just feel like doing it again. Like the right pair of shoes, the perfect haircut will fit you like a glove, add bounce to your step, and keep on looking good through miles of wear.

Hang

Hang up a jacket, two raincoats, a snowsuit, three backpacks, a baseball cap you've never seen before, and a couple of bathing suits. Hang the sleeping bag out on the line after finding it wadded up in a wet ball in the cellar. Hang some kind of air freshener in your son's room and hang his socks as far away as you can. Hang herbs and flowers upside-down in the attic to dry, then make your own potpourri. Hang up the phone while you're making lunch, before your neck and shoulders start to hang all funny. Take those pictures and papers and collages out of the garage and hang them in a makeshift gallery going up the stairs. Hang that picture of your second cousin three times removed, who was a movie star once for five minutes. On April Fools' Day, when the kids hang your bras from the old maple tree, hang out the white flag and hang loose for a while.

Harmony

Every family's bound to have squabbles. Even the
Brady Bunch. Especially yours. Tempers will flare
and hurtful words will fly and sometimes tension
will claim the air like a thunderstorm that just
won't break. Still, harmony is a worthwhile
pursuit. Mutual kindness and common courtesy
are fine things to have around a house. When
everyone's on the same page, humming the same
tune, you can make beautiful music together. (At
least you can share the same stage.) So what's the
problem? You've got one very loud voice that
demands to be heard above all the others. One
player wants to be first violin, and there are
already two others ahead of him. If you've got a
prima donna, give her the starring role. When
everybody's squawking off-key, someone's got to
carry the melody. And the laws of harmony say
it's probably you.

Harvest

What joy there is in reaping the harvest! After tilling the soil, preparing the rows, and planting seeds, you finally taste the fruits of your labor. For years, you carried your child from specialist to specialist, and at last found someone who helped him to speak. And in those precious words lay your harvest. You tried to conceive, and after every test you could imagine and every indignity and every new procedure, you cradled a newborn in your arms. In that moment, you reaped what you had sown. Not every seed you plant is the fast-sprouting kind. Not every soil you plant in is rich, fertile loam. Sometimes you must move through long years of inner exploration, before the outer world can acknowledge the truth of who you are. It seems like forever that you tend and you water and trim back the weeds that threaten your growth. Trust! In time, a rich bounty you'll harvest!

Have

The goal is not how much you have, but what you gain on the way to obtain it. What good is having it all, if you have learned nothing that helps you to use what you have? What's the point of having a generous heart if you're too shut down to share it? Who cares if you have the voice of an angel if you lack the courage to sing out loud? Your ease with foreign languages serves no one if you can't step beyond your comfort zone and engage with different cultures. You have been blessed with talents that are yours and yours alone. Only you have your ability to mediate conflict. Only you have your humor; only you have that smile. Now you have a child and what an opportunity you have! To pass on your gifts and share all that you have.

Healing

A mother's journey is to heal. From the moment you begin to contemplate life with children, you will come face to face with your thorniest unresolved issues. You will uncover ancient hurts around your own childhood and the mothering that was given you (or not). Embrace this singular opportunity for healing. Remain open to a flood of emotions, and flow with them until you find a healing peace. Give yourself room to heal and know that you heal for those who came before you and those who now follow. Create new endings to old, tired stories of loss and betrayal. Inspire your children with new legacies and new, life-affirming ways. Take bold steps to change painful patterns passed down through generations. Seek out the medicine that strengthens you and take authority for your own healing. Every mother who heals herself, heals her children, too.

Heart

Live from your heart at least as often as you live from your head. Feel your heart open wider every time you gaze upon your sleeping child. Every time you see yourself in the way she stands with her hand on her hip or her finger slicing the air. Fill every day with red hearts and pink hearts decorated with glitter and sparkle and "I Luv U" scrawled across the front. Give from the heart without conditions and teach your children to do the same. Love from the heart without strings and let love return the same way. In every decision, listen to your heart. Place your hand lightly over your heart and check in. How does your heart feel? What is it saying? Pull down the walls you've built around your heart. Soften the tough, protective layers you've let grow around your heart. Be willing to act from the heart again and again—no matter how many times it's been broken.

Heartache

It comes with the territory. Once you open your mother-heart wide, you leave yourself open to heartache. Every time your child stumbles, your heart skips a beat. Every pain your child feels, you feel, too. Children move on and your heart starts breaking. You lose a child too early; the ache never stops. You share all your passions and they choose their own, and a part of your heart starts to crumble. You know it's bound to happen, you think that you're ready, yet it feels like an ambush all the same. Your sweet, perfect baby walks a path shrouded in shadow. Nothing you can do stems the heartache. Thirteen years without a phone call or even a card, and your heart melts a bit more each day. Some mothers live with it all of their days. It feels hollow and empty. Like heartache.

Heaven

Heaven is a baby's breath warm against your shoulder. There's a celestial grace in lying skin-to-skin with a very small person who looks astonishingly like you. A nap in the sun is a sweet slice of heaven, especially when you're curled up with someone you love. A heavenly whisper under the stars reminds you how close are the angels. A rainbow arching across the sky—and you feel transported to a heavenly realm. You know you're in heaven when the cherries are ripe—and you're doubly sure with your first, juice-filled bite. Heaven is a kiss, a glance, a lingering sigh. A fragrant bouquet tinged with lilac. What mother hasn't surmised that heaven is near, when the first gentle "Mama" makes its way to her ears? Heaven is a moment right here on earth: two people in love, a baby, a birth.

Help

If you think you can carry off this mothering thing without help, you most definitely need help. Get used to the idea of asking for it without shame, receiving it without a hint of hesitation, and graciously accepting it whenever it's offered. Pay handsomely for it if you must. If you can. Seek help from young people and old people, from professionals and well-meaning amateurs, from friends of family and family of friends. Most definitely, seek help from above. Post "Help Wanted" messages on the Internet and on the bulletin board at the laundromat, and at the local college. Don't fool yourself into believing you can do it all. When you start getting snappy with the children, it's a call for help. When you bring out the wail of the martyr, it's a scream for help. Get over yourself and find yourself some help! Heaven help the mother who's too proud to cry, "Help!"

Here

This is the place where you feel most at home.
Here, where you conceived your babies. Here,
where the water meets the shore. Here in the land
of your mother's mother's mother. If you can
make a life here, you can make one anywhere.
Here, in front of the bright April moon. This is
the site of your takeoff; here is where you return.
Here, underneath the old sycamore. Here where
the blueberries grow wild. Your children are not
from this place, but you are. Here where wild
mustangs once ran free. Here, beside the sleeping
rainbow. Here, where you found a twisted root
that told you the tale of your future. Here is your
crossroad. Here you can grow. When you find
what is here, you'll learn what you're after. Everything that matters to a mother is here.

Hold

Hold everything. Hold on to the memory of how
it felt to hold your baby the very first time. Hold
hands before crossing the street and before
offering grace. Hold tight when the carousel first
starts to turn. Hold on to the reins of your
horsey! Hold a space in your heart for your trou-
bled child. Hold a space where you see her get
well. Hold a vigil and ask all her friends to hold a
white candle. Hold on to the house as long as you
can—then let it go. Hold a snake; it's not really
slimy. Hold your lover in a passionate embrace.
Hold a child in your lap while the child holds a
bunny. Hold the mayo, hold the onions. Hold the
elevator! Hold yourself accountable for your
actions, and hold others to the same standards.
When you reach out for a grab-hold and find
there is none, let go of the impulse to hold on.

Home

No matter how much or how far you migrate, a mother needs a place to call home. It could be a tiny studio in the city, a five-bedroom home in the suburbs, or a customized RV that's tricked out and ready to roll. Home is where the kids can find you even when they're grown with kids of their own. Home is where you keep the first-grade drawings and the third-grade dream-catchers and the pictures from the fifth-grade dance. When you can run naked from the shower to the laundry, you're home. When you know precisely where to find the cookie cutters shaped like fruit, you're home. Wherever you brought the baby when you left the hospital, no matter how briefly you stayed there, will always feel like home. If pressed, moms can live for weeks out of a suitcase and backpack their way down the Appalachian Trail. Yet when all is said and done, a mom needs a door and a jubilant voice crying, "Mom! Where are you? I'm home!"

Honor

Honor yourself for the mother you are and others will honor you, too. Acknowledge that you have always done the very best you could in any moment, and honor that next time you may do differently. Honor your patience when you are exhausted. Honor your resiliency when you are stretched raw and frayed thin. Honor your past, warts and all, for it brought you to where you are today. Honor another mother's journey, too, including the woman who mothered you. For under the surface we are all the same. Honor her tears as well as her silence. Her tenacity as well as her ability to let go. Her decision to stay home full-time or half-time, to parent alone or with a partner or with a family that doesn't look anything like yours. Honor every mother's journey, for under the surface we are all the same. When you honor the best you can see in a mother, remember to bestow the same honor on you.

Hope

For the sake of the children, be hopeful. Hope
they inherit a world of peace. Hope that by the
time they are the leaders, greed and power will
hold no sway. Raise their hopes—and hope that
they'll never be shattered. In all things, set
hopeful intentions. Instill your child with a sense
of promise and a deep yearning for a culture
where judgment cannot stand. Fill their hearts
with the knowing that we are all one earth family:
people, rivers, animals, trees. Hope they do no
harm. When you walk your talk of cooperation,
hope that someone is watching where your steps
go. When you transform your words of trust into
faithful actions, hope they all notice the love in
your eyes. Hope that the worst is over and that
the best is yet to be. Carry the light of hope for
us all. Especially, hope for the children.

How

It's so good to breathe out and let go of the *how*.
How is it supposed to be done? How do you
know it's right? How do you decide? How can this
possibly happen? You know how to be a good
mother, whether or not you know how you know
it. See yourself reaching your goals without
knowing just how you will get there. Commit to
an intention and begin taking steps—without
needing to know how it all will turn out. Even for
a moment or a day, free yourself from the burden
of figuring out every detail of how, when, and
where. Trust that your job is not always understanding the *how*. The answer will come as soon
as you acknowledge that there's a way it can
happen—whether or not you know how. There
are forces at work that you don't need to master.
Just trust that they work, and don't fret over how.

Hugs

Have you had your hugs today? Have you wrapped your arms around another and felt your souls touch for a tender moment? Hugs bring us closer together in more ways than the physical. Coming heart-to-heart for a mutual embrace speaks of trust and affection between two human beings. Besides, it feels so good! Hugs ask you to breathe in unison with someone you care for, and to be vulnerable enough to connect below the surface. Hugs come in all shapes and sizes: big, belly-bumping bear hugs; polite, kiss-the-air hugs; and juicy, meaty, mommy hugs that make everything OK. When the night is really dark, baby needs a hug. When the report cards come out, Mr. Know-It-All needs hugs. After a day when the washer blew, the computer went down, and everybody was running with the runs, Mom needs group hugs galore. There's a lot a mom can go without, but don't forget the hugs!

Humor

Although mothers have a refined sense of smell, it's their sense of humor they've honed to perfection. Did you hear the one about the mother who locked herself in the bathroom on March 30 and didn't come out until the taxes were done? Did you hear the one about the three kids, the blender without a top, and six pounds of apple brown Betty? There's a reason everybody loved Lucy and almost nobody got down with Mommie Dearest. There's nothing as sad as a humorless mom. She stalks the night tight-lipped and shoulders hunched, pacing about and scanning the landscape and daring anyone to find humor in her wretched existence. Put the woman out of her misery and toss a banana peel squarely in her path. Touch up her face with a mask of meringue and tickle her feet with buffalo feathers. Mothers are at the center of one cosmic joke—but we're asleep when they get to the punch line.

Imagination

Imagine yourself in a world of untold beauty. You rest in the arms of comfort and joy. Imagine you have everything you ever want, with no struggle, no worry or pain. Imagine there is no such feeling as fear. Imagine a peace that radiates from every heart and surrounds the entire world. Imagine the trees laden with delicious fruits: pomegranate, mango, papaya, and orange. The crystal waters flow from high on the mountains and collect in sparkling ponds and lakes that are home to glorious, rainbow-hued fish. The fields are green and fertile. Imagine a violet light coming into you and filling you with a presence that you know to be love. Imagine that presence moving out to your fingertips, passing on to every being you touch. Imagine love passed from mother to father, to children, to friends. Imagine that what you see in your imagination is actually already here.

Improvise

If you can't remember where you filed the instructions that came with your child, make it up as you go. If you don't have a clue, punt. You'll still be one step ahead of the crowd. Take in all the information you want, then jazz it up with a little spice of your own. Listen to the advice of elders you trust, then update their rhythm so it rocks to the beat of your own drum. Check out the handmade toys at $69.95, then make your own. Flip through the catalogs to see what they're doing with T-shirts, then get out the paint box and color some up. Leave out the pork and add portobellos, and call it whatever you want. Sometimes the best way to get where you need to go is to throw away the map and ignore all the signs. Try this way, then that, then this way again. Things may not turn out exactly as planned, but you can be sure that something will happen.

Independence

The more you make a stand for your own independence, the faster your child will take steps to declare hers. You're not really fused at the hip, though it may feel that way. Your child need not cling to you all of his life, though you may foster that even as you say you never will. Cut the cord and find the freedom that is yours. Then watch everyone around you find his or her own independence. They can arrange their own rides and make their own sandwiches. Fix their own bikes and wash their own sheets. As they earn your trust, they'll earn independence. And they can start earning some spending money, too. A household of independent thinkers cooperates more and fights for territory less. They learn to stand on their own two feet without stepping on others' toes. At first you might feel that you've been left behind. But you've only claimed your right to true independence.

Insight

Just on the other side of intuition lies insight. Not only do you know what you know. You have a sense of why you know it. Your understanding surpasses the facts and figures laid out before you. Your vision extends beyond mere sight. Insight invites you to look a little further and a little deeper, until you feel the pieces click together in a richer, rounder way. When you gain insight, your perspective broadens. Possibility expands. Where others see a child having a temper tantrum, you see an explosion of fear and frustration. When some mothers feel that everything is ending, your insight illumines a wave of beginnings. What you see on the surface is the tip of an iceberg, and insight allows you to navigate safely around it without crashing into a deep blue unknown. It's not always more thinking that carries us through; it's the picture we draw from our insight.

Insist

Insist that others hold true to their agreements.
Insist the same for yourself. If a move is afoot to
play fast and loose with the truth, insist that the
game has now ended. Insist that the circle be wide
enough to include everyone. Insist that each voice
will be heard. Insist that your children wear seat
belts, even for the shortest ride. If you're lucky,
they'll insist that you buckle up, too. If the work
was shoddy the first time around, insist that they
do it all over. Insist that, this time, it's done right.
You can do all you want to insist you get respect,
but the only way it works is that you earn it.
Insist that the store take back the sweater that
started unraveling the very first day that you wore
it. If they give you a hard time, be insistent.

Instant

Instant pudding, instant pie. Soup you can make in the wink of an eye. You'd cook from scratch— but why even try? Why not go instant today? Instant cash at the ATM. Instant E-mails you send to a friend. You've hardly just started and here comes the end. Everything's instant today! Results that are instant. Here before tomorrow. Seeking a mortgage? Five minutes 'til you borrow. Here's something that instantly wipes away sorrow. Instant is the happening way. Wash out this shirt and it's dry in a flash. Need instant credit? It's faster than cash. Just water up these flakes. No potatoes to mash! It's instant. No waiting today. Instant family, instant life. Sometimes you feel like an instant wife. Forget presized portions and pick up a knife. Does it have to be instant today?

Instinct

Instead of information, try instinct. Listen to the part of yourself that always has known how to mother. Animals in the wild don't read a lot of books, and yet the females are born knowing how to raise their young. A mother eagle knows when it's time to push her babies out of the nest, and it's her instinctual calendar that tells her. If you're wondering whether to put a jacket on baby, walk outside and feel the temperature. If going to movies makes everyone cranky, no psychologist needs to tell you to stop. Too much input from too many sources will rob you of your maternal instinct. You'll stop listening because there's nothing to hear. Give your instinct a chance to flourish. Nurture it with quiet time to call up your own wisdom. Tend it with sufficient trust to act on your answers. And trust your own instinct to know when you're right.

Intuition

If you could bottle and sell mothers' intuition, I have a feeling you would soon be a millionaire. Moms have a way of knowing what no one else could know. You can be staring at a stoplight and suddenly your gut tells you that someone's got a headache—and the school nurse calls twenty minutes later. You're brushing your teeth and the weirdest sensation suggests that something's not right with your uncle. You turn on the TV and watch the towers fall. Your intuition is a powerful early warning system not to ignore. When something tells you to check on the baby, do so. If you have an inkling to E-mail an old friend, don't delay. When the small voice within says to drive downtown, trust your instincts without knowing why. There's a lot to be gleaned from your own intuition, but, of course, you already know.

Invest

Find something worth investing in. Do it for the financial payback or the emotional payback or simply for the sheer joy of watching something grow. Buy CDs or buy stocks or buy shares in a community co-op market. Invest in a friend's new business idea. Invest your time and your energy and your unconditional support. Buy an old house that needs tender, loving care and invest hours and hours of sweat equity. Get clear about the currency that matters most to you, and the dreams that live in your heart. Invest in your child's future by planting trees or building stock portfolios or collecting something that your gut tells you will be more valuable tomorrow than it is today. Invest in your own well-being and know you'll always come out ahead. Invest in your health. Invest in more education or more training or invest in some healing that you've felt yourself needing for a long time. The wisest investment you can ever make is the investment you make in yourself.

Invitations

Your sister just called and asked you to a party.
The neighbors are having potluck and they want
you to attend. Your daughter was invited to the
lake for a weekend, and you can go fishing, too.
Who doesn't love invitations? They come by mail
in brightly flowered envelopes that spill out
confetti when opened. They pop up on your
E-mail bordered by balloons and bulldogs wearing
bows. No matter who gets one or how it arrives,
everybody's excited. Tickets to the season
opener—and they're paid for! Backstage passes
and you get to the meet the band. The gallery's
hanging a brand-new exhibit—and guess who's
invited to show? You're besieged with requests to
share your slide show, and the women's luncheon
series wants to host you next spring. Though you
might be too tired to accept them with pleasure,
receiving the invitation is the next best thing.

Journey

Your life is a journey. It will take you from mountain to desert, from fertile fields to dusty plains. At times you may feel lost and unsure of your way, but the journey will always continue. Even when you feel that everything has stopped, that you must be going in the wrong direction, that, too, is a part of your journey. You may travel alone for miles, and then join up with companions. The road will fork and some will leave your company never to be heard from again. Journeys never follow the shortest distance between two points. They wind and twist and meander, and the scenery changes year after year. A mother's journey traverses a lush and many-faceted landscape. When you grow tired of the journey, when you are disheartened and feel that you cannot go on, find a place to rest and be nourished. Come back to your heart, touch the reasons you continue. Take time to marvel at this journey you're on.

Joy

More than a feeling and deeper than any emotion, joy is a pure state of being. Joy is holding your child to your breast for the very first time and locking lovers' eyes. Joy is being in love and sleeping in the sunshine and running down a mountain path with the swiftness of a deer in the springtime. Joy expands your heart and opens your soul until you know, really know, that death is simply the turning of another page. Joy is snowflakes and slipping on the ice and getting up so you can slip all over again and never even feeling the cold. Living in joy doesn't mean putting on a happy face. It means that joy is at the core of who you are and always have been. Joy is strong enough to carry you through the darkness and the pain into a place where joy still resides in ultimate measure. Seek to find joy and let joy fill your life.

Juicy

Let the juices flow! Mothers need a steady diet of juice. Not the kind that comes in bags and pouches, but the inner juices of a woman living a rich and succulent life. Creative juices that pour out a river of self-expression. You know a juicy mom when you see her. She's a bit out on the edge, pushing up against boundaries that she's outgrowing by the minute. A juicy mom's not afraid to get down on the floor with her children and undulate a snake walk. She'll be the first one to volunteer to juice up the classroom with her songs and stories. Her inspirational juices are always on tap. She shines a little brighter than others around her; spills out her juicy delicious lightness on everyone she sees. She's out on the dance floor with the teenagers, and she moves like there's juice from her head to her knees. Come on Mom, how juicy can you be?

Kiss

Keep on kissing. Plant those tiny butterfly kisses on tiny little baby toes and sweet little toddler necks and bumpy teenager foreheads. Kiss the back of a hand or the bottom of a (clean) foot, a balding head, or a wet puppy mouth. Kiss good morning, good night, goodbye, good luck. Kiss boo-boos and teary eyes and tender ears and pictures of people you can't kiss in person anymore. Tuck chocolate kiss candies into lunch bags and pink kiss notes into pockets and send E-mail kisses and voice mail kisses and envelopes stuffed with cutouts of your own kissable lips. If you're being disrespected, tell your boss to kiss off and kiss that job goodbye! In the middle of a busy day, find time for kissing. An apple a day may keep the doctor away, but what keeps your heart strong is more kissing!

Kitchen

Mom always admitted there was no place that she'd rather be. She kept her copper-bottom cookware hanging in perfect order, small to large and pots to pans. She knew the location of every spice and every spoon and could find them with her eyes shut tight. The woman had a special gift for pulling things out of cupboards and refrigerator doors and deep freezes, and transforming them into a feast fit for the gods. How did she ever learn it all? She never consulted a cookbook, never took notes from a television chef. She shooed everybody out and descended into a deep state of concentration. When the steam slipped out into the hallway and the flavors wafted into the den, we knew it was only a matter of minutes. The kitchen was her stage, and she never stopped performing. My mom could do a lot of things, but boy, could she cook!

Know

Mothers don't know everything, but luckily their children don't know that. You know what you know, you know? You may not know a whole lot about medicine, but you know when your child is not well. You may not know the law, but you know when it feels like your rights have been trampled. When someone tells you every child should know how to read before entering first grade, answer, "Really? I don't think I knew that." Learn the difference between what you know— and what you believe. Truth is, what you don't know can hurt you. Your child may know her favorite cartoon theme story, but does she know the name of her neighbor next door? Does your teen know too much about sex, or do you fear that he knows much too little? You know a lot more than you might think you know. Only you know if you know how to use it.

Laugh

Who ever said that mothering is such a serious job? Gather your children around you, roar like hyenas, and laugh! Sweet, gurgling giggles, out-loud guffaws, and basso profundo belly laughs. What else can you do while you scrape baby vomit from in between the floorboards—using nothing but your scraggly fingernails? What could be more appropriate when faced with a dog, a plateful of burgers fresh off the grill, and a powerful canine appetite? When your choice is to laugh or cry, why not go with a combo? Roll on the floor and show everyone around you the beauty of laughing out loud. Laugh until the tears roll down your cheeks and your sides ache. While the rest of the sourpusses wait to see who has the laugh last, you'll be tickled to know that you tossed out the first!

Laundry

Not so much the doing it, but the knowing that it's done. Whatever it takes to get there is worth the trip. Piles of blueberry-stained shorts and mud-stained dresses and dust-clogged jeans transformed. Bibs and bandanas dug out from backpacks; underwear recovered from behind hampers and anywhere else they've been flung. White cotton diapers returned to purity. Stacks of towels folded, shirts on hangers, and tiny socks reunited with mates. Little pullovers and big sweatshirts and silken things that nearly slip through your hands. Zippers zipped. Buttons buttoned. Warm from the dryer or fresh from the clothesline, these are the things that lie against the skin of your loved ones every single day. Laundry is a kaleidoscope of texture, color, smell, and touch. In your rush to get through as fast as you can, remember to savor the sensations. And to feel how good it is when laundry is done.

Leap

Once you warm up with baby steps, you're ready
to take your next leap. Take a leap of faith and
know you can make it. Decide to leap over tall
buildings with a single bound. Close your eyes
and open your own business. Take the leap!
March yourself into the recovery center and tell
them you're ready to heal. Make your leap! Take a
leap into a second marriage and take the kids
with you. Leap off the edge of your personal zone
of comfort and feel the feelings you've been
stuffing for years. Tired of small-town living?
Leap into something larger. Frustrated by fear in
the city? Leap over the freeway and onto a farm.
You're ready for the big stage and you know it, so
take your leap. You can't keep playing small
forever. Take your leap! Keep your eyes on the
prize. Let your feet touch the skies. Take a hard
running start. Now leap!

Leave

There will come a time when you really must leave. Not forever, but for an hour or so. You'll leave your oldest in charge and you'll leave the dishes half done, and you'll just make like a tree and leave. You'll leave because you have to go. Because you can't stay. Because something about that moment is sucking the life out of you and you are compelled to go and retrieve it. You don't have to leave in anger; you simply have to leave. Leave with a smile on your lips and a cheery "Goodbye." You can go to a movie or a mall or a meadow. Go alone or go with a friend. It's not so important where you are headed. What matters is that you be gone. You can leave the dryer going: someone will hear it. You can leave the movie on: someone will watch it. When you come back, you can pick up where you left off. But first, before anything, get up and leave.

Legacy

The best that you leave your children will never fit into a hope chest. Let your legacy be kindness and compassion. Let them remember the way you always offered a helping hand from a true and giving heart. Leave your children knowing that everyone makes mistakes, and the real test is how you correct them. Create a legacy of self-care rather than self-sacrifice. Let it be said that you passed along the keys to a full-spectrum life rooted in unconditional love and a deep dance with spirit. That you spent a lifetime asking questions and seeking answers and knowing you might never find them. Let future generations inherit the understanding that when every being takes its place in the circle of life, harmony will prevail over all. What greater gift to leave behind than a glorious life well-lived? If that is the legacy that carries your name, you've left them all rich beyond means.

Less

Yes, you can get by with less. Less work to do if you share it with others. Less time to do it when you're having more fun. Try eating less food that's less likely to leave you less nourished. Let yourself be less than perfect, and discover that others will criticize you less. Less television and everyone's a bit less lethargic. Fewer mindless hours surfing the Net probably breeds a lot less contempt. Less stuff. Less clutter. A lot less mess. Fewer trips to the mall and you'll bring home less of what you don't need. And you really do need so much less! Less rush. Less worry. Less fear. Less stress. Working less. Dressing less. Lunching less. Crunching less. There's so much more to do with less. Time expands greatly when you fill it with less. Space is serene when it's asked to hold less. There's untold abundance at the center of less. All around, less is more, more or less.

Let

Let go of anything that's become too heavy. Let yourself have a break. Let him go. Let her go. Let them go and know they'll do fine. Let her spike her hair—who's it going to hurt? Let them paint their rooms any color they want (as long as they let you approve). Let the cake cool before frosting. Let that pan soak overnight. "Will somebody please let the cat out?" Let bygones be bygones and let the dead rest in peace. "Can you please just let up a little?" "Can you let him have another chance?" "Why can't you just let it be?" Let them work it out themselves. Don't let yourself get caught in the middle. Let go and let God. Let sleeping dogs lie. Open the windows and let a little sunshine in. Let there be peace on Earth. Let it begin with you.

Letters

You know how you love to get letters. They don't have to be overly eloquent, and you're willing to let go of bad grammar just this once. You love them penned on monogrammed stationery and scrawled on pages ripped from a school notebook. The best ones have hand-colored doodles on the envelope, with more continued inside. They go on for days with newsy news, and the pen color changed every time the writer put it away. You still have the first letter she sent home after leaving for college. You kept it in your bedside drawer for years, taking it out every so often and imagining your baby studying in the library and going to a sorority mixer. When the men were away, you held your breath for the letters. Short sentences told of unfamiliar cultures and fear in the dark, and always asked how the children were helping you cope. When you can't reach across the table and lay your hand on a loved one, you're thankful for letters that keep you in touch.

Libido

Your sex life is not gone, it is just away. Wherever you think your libido might have run off to, it will be back. Believe it or not, the day will come when you will feel surges of passion again, when you will find your partner exceedingly attractive once more, when you will remember that baby-making is a means, not just an end. Right now, you may find it hard to differentiate between hot sex and wet sox. Quiet attempts at arousal may be no match for your snoring. As remote as it appears, the time will come when you will gladly trade hours of uninterrupted sleep for long, languid lovemaking under a low-hung crescent moon. As outrageous as it may now seem, the phrase "Oh, Baby!" will take on new meaning. The adults will reclaim the night. The morning. The afternoon. And your libido? Missing in action no more.

Lift

Lift the baby out of the car seat and lift her into the swing. Lift the groceries out of the car and lift them onto the kitchen counter. Moms are heavyweights when it comes to lifting. Lift up the edge of the sofa and discover why the outside ants are coming in. Lift up those leaky boxes in the garage and immediately wish you hadn't. Is there no end to the lifting? Lift the blinds and hope the dazzling sun will lift your teenager out of an unrousable sleep. Lift that six-year-old while you still can. Do your best to lift everybody's spirits when the trip to the amusement park is ruined by the rain. Lift your own when the deal falls through—again. Lift hockey's biggest fan on your shoulders so he can see the game. When the clouds have lifted and the worst is behind you, lift your glass to the heavens and lift your voice in grateful song.

Lighten

Lighten up! Lighten your schedule by saying, "Thanks, but no thanks" to committees and fund-raisers and socializing that drags you down instead of lightening you up. Don't take everything so seriously: the world will continue to turn even if your toddler wears one green striped sock, one red flowered sock, and his shirt inside out. Clear out your purse and stop lugging around things you never need. Get rid of old clothes that nobody ever wears, and lighten up the ordeal of morning dressing. Let go of old resentments and old emotional baggage and feel your spirits lighten up. Lighten up, Mom! Don't fret so much about sparkling clean faces and perfectly combed hair and fingerprints on the bathroom mirror. Save some energy for the important things. Okay, so she left her jacket on the bus again. So you got to work and there was peanut butter smeared on your skirt! If you saw it in a movie, you'd think it was funny. Your world isn't quite such a burdensome place, so take a tip from the angels and lighten!

Limit

If you don't set limits for your child, who will?
Limit the amount of time in front of the television, limit the noise, limit the sugar and the soda
and anything that limits the possibility of peace
and quiet. Don't go hog wild; just set some limits.
Before you add one more art class or one more
soccer season, think about whether a too-full
schedule limits your child's opportunity to dream,
to wonder, to do nothing at all. Set limits for
yourself, too. Cut back on the number of times
you say, "Oh, I'd be happy to," and feel the
freedom that comes from saying, "No, I don't
think that's going to work for me." When you
start to ask whether you're paying too much
attention to your own well-being, remember that
the sky's the limit when it comes to self-care.

Listen

Listen to the sounds of happy children playing, then listen to the sound of your smile. When your child is bursting to tell you something, listen. When she refuses to say anything at all, listen more closely than ever. Even when you're so tired you can barely keep your eyes open, listen when your teenager wants to talk about his day. Always, always, always listen to your own intuition. Today, listen to a different radio station. When the birds are outside your window greeting the day, take the time to listen. Lie down and listen to the music of your own beating heart. Listen! Did you hear something? Listen! Did he just say "Mama"? Listen! Was that at last a yawn? Listen and hear yourself speaking the words you need to say—speaking your truth so others will listen.

Lists

Who gets dropped off where and picked up when. Which store has the organic rice milk, which has that string cheese the kids love, and which has the best prices on oven-roasted turkey breast. Which baby-sitters will stay overnight and which ones never will. What are everybody's sock and shoe sizes this month. School phone tree. Church phone tree. Soccer team phone tree. Scouts phone tree. Short list of PG-13 movies that the twins can see; much longer list of the ones they can't. Passwords for the Internet, for the security system, for the automatic sprinkler, for the DVD, VCR, ATM. Cell phone numbers. Work numbers. Home numbers. Pager numbers. Who's allergic to what. What restaurants have a Kids Eat Free policy (long list). What adult-only motels have a hot tub in every room (short list).

Love

Suddenly, all you need is love. Hours of endless gazing into your beloved's eyes. The sweet-soft nuzzle of your dear one's cheek against your own, and sugar-tinged kissies that can melt the frostiest morning. Did you ever imagine that one tiny human being could utterly enchant you so? Could you have seen yourself so infatuated with visits to the potty and tiny bootprints in the snow? It feels as though you could never open your heart wide enough to take in all the joy and all the challenge that parenting brings. Yet when you do, you will get lost in love and find yourself anew. This is mother's deep and endless love. Father's tender-hearted love. It carries you aloft through tumble-down days and teething nights, and into the unspeakable delight of finding that first red-crayoned valentine scribble on the wall. Beneath the tears, the hopes and fears, love is all there is.

Magic

When my mother wasn't sure how things would work out, she'd always leave it up to the magic. Then she'd sit and wait for the magic to come. We never really believed in it, but somehow she always pulled a rabbit right out of that hat. When money was tight, someone would stop by with a roast and some homemade lasagna. Just like that. When the baby's fever wouldn't break, Mom would disappear into the kitchen and come back with her magic fairy water and before you knew it, the baby would be sound asleep. It just happened. Mom always had a twinkle in her eye when she called on the magic. It wasn't like she waved magic wands or made incantations or did anything that would freak out the neighbors. I can't really say what she did or just how she did it. It was just Mom and her magic, I guess.

Make

Make dinner every night for a month and then pick up the phone and make reservations. At the museum, make an Indian dream-catcher with feathers and beads, and put it over the bed for peaceful sleeping. Make amends for that bit of displeasure with your own mother. Make an apology if it's yours to make. Make a ludicrous offer on the house on the corner and then make it your best home ever. Make it work for everyone involved. Make a vow to make fresh berry pies when the fruits are in season. Make new friends—lots of them—and make your days and nights richer all around. Make sure the baby gate is up and make certain that the fire is out. Make your own stencils of stars and sprinkle them across a blue ceiling. Make angels in the snow and then make a wish. Make a promise. Make a life. Make it yours.

Marvel

Marvel at the magic of being a mother. Amaze yourself with your ability to see through eyes in the back of your head. To know exactly how many chocolate chips were left at 1:33, and how many were eaten by the time 3:45 rolled around. Astound yourself with your psychic abilities. How your intuition tells you when something is not right, even before a word is spoken. How you can tell when someone is trying to play fast and loose with the truth, simply by the way she twists her hair in that trademark spiral motion. How can you observe your child learning to say "Mama" or proving the Pythagorean theorem or riding a horse—and not just feel yourself overcome with the absolute, marvelous miracle of life? How you can hurry past nature without noticing? How can you look in your mirror and not marvel?

Massage

Here are ten reasons why it's time for you to get a massage: Because you carry thirty-five pounds of child on your hip every day and your load is only getting heavier. Because after an eighteen-hour day, you stay up at the computer into the wee hours, working on your first novel and working your neck and shoulders into a tizzy. Because you deserve a full hour where the focus is all about you and the music is as soft and sweet as a lullaby. Because your back has never been quite the same since you moved the sofa bed in a rearranging frenzy. Because all you have to do is lie there. Because the gift certificate expires in three days and your sister-in-law will never forgive you if you waste it. Because you're starving to be touched without having to touch back. Because you want to thank your body for all it does for you every single day. Because you want it, plain and simple. Because once this massage is over, you can schedule yourself for the next.

Meander

Pay attention to a child and you can master meandering. Who knows better how to transform a quick trip to the post office into a forty-five-minute excursion highlighted by the discovery of a cracked robin's egg on the sidewalk, a detour past some very seductive swings, and an impromptu engagement with a friendly Chihuahua? If you have a list of seven errands and a tight time frame, you'd best find a way to go it alone. With a child, even crossing the street becomes an adventure. Let's go over here to see how the trash truck works! Look over there! Is that a balloon? Moms need more meandering. When you let yourself meander, you discover that tiny tortilla place you never saw before. You just might be the first ones to see the baby ducklings down by the pond. The shortest distance between two points might get the job done, but meandering gives the trip meaning. Haven't you been meaning to meander?

Memories

First bicycle. First kiss. First period. Last day of school. Be prepared for an unending flood of memories as your children grow. Remember yourself at that age, overwhelmed by those sensations, stepping over another threshold. How do you welcome your memories? Gingerly, steeling yourself for old hurts? Or joyfully, with the softer eyes that come with age? Choose the version of the past that most supports your present. Choose the memory that makes you smile, brings a flush to your cheeks, sets your body atingle. Don't deny the rest; just send them on their way. Show your child how good it feels to remember what the heart can never forget. Share the memories that can help build a better future, that can shift everyone into more loving ways. You and you alone are the author of your story. Remember: you are the keeper of the tale that is you.

Mobilize

Harness the phenomenal power of mothers and make something happen. Put together your minds and your hearts and mobilize for issues that matter. March for more equitable child care and access to health care. Raise awareness and raise consciousness and, yes, raise big money. Mobilize and realize there's power in numbers. Gather legions of moms who insist that no child go hungry, that schools offer more than standardized testing, and that babies take priority over bombs. Build a groundswell of support for training mothers who want to work and transforming lives of welfare into well-being. Create a mothers' lobby and move moms into Congress. Channel the passion for peace that mothers share. Mothers united are moms moving mountains. Dust off your politics and mobilize, moms!

Moderation

Goldilocks was a guru for moderation. Never satisfied with *too this* or *too that*, she always held out for *just right*. In between the polarities of all or nothing, feast or famine, black or white, love or hate, rests a wide river of moderation. Why crash up against the rocks on either side when you can let the gentle current in the center carry you along? Why jump in way over your head, or barely dip in a toe, when you could be enjoying the pleasures of a knee-deep wade? There's no wisdom in dismissing something completely—and missing out on the gems that it may contain. Why punctuate your policies with *never!* when you could reap the benefits of *once in a while* and still hold true to principle? Like Goldilocks, opt for the middle way, and emerge rested and fed.

Moments

Stay aware or you'll miss the moments. They come without warning, and if you're too busy talking on your cell phone or communing with the computer, you might miss them altogether. Blink twice, and the moment may be gone. It can be as fleeting as a butterfly on a fingertip. A look of delight as a pony passes by. The glimmer of recognition upon seeing Grammy and Poppa for the second time. There's a moment when you know your baby belongs to the world, and it's a swift and powerful moment. You're nursing your infant and she turns as if to say "I'm done," and that's a moment of ending that won't return. Your child is with you and then he's gone, and the moment never goes away. A lifetime is made of a series of moments. Pass up the moments and life passes you by.

Mommy

Not every mother's a mommy. Mommies drag out bags and boxes of fabric scraps and ribbon, and make little dolls out of socks. They climb up on the jungle gym right beside you and never once say, "Be careful." Mother gives you pizza on a plate with a knife and a fork, but Mommy just opens the box. Mommies skip with you hand-in-hand. They sit on the curb with you to watch the parade and would never bother bringing a chair. Mommies want to do their hair just like yours. Mommies would always rather walk than drive. When mommies do ring-around-the-rosy, they fall all the way down at the end. Mommy sleeps curled up with you like a spoon, especially if the movie was scary. Mommy knows more elephant jokes than even a kid, and Mommy knows best how to tell them.

More

You want more quiet and they want more noise.
You want more reading and they want more toys.
He wants more girls and you want more boys.
What more could Mom ever ask for? Maybe more
sleep and more time to herself. More closets and
bathrooms and more kitchen shelves. More help
with the laundry. More help after school. How
much more of this pooping? How much more of
this drool? You want more adventure. They crave
more routine. You'd like some more babies and
now you've got teens! They all want more chocolate and you want more greens. What more could
Mom ever ask for? You've got lots more kissies
and lots more hugs, too. Your heart is more open.
Your blues are more blue. You've got much more
to live for and so much more to do. What more
could Mom ever ask for?

Move

When nothing is moving, everything dies. Move into more intimacy with your beloved and keep love alive. Move away from old patterns of abandonment and fear. Move out of your head and into your heart. Clean up the old garage and move the car and move into your brand-new office. Pack up your things and move into the house you already live in. Move the furniture and the paintings and move the mirror for better feng shui. Move like a child. Crawl and skip and twirl and hop on one foot. Don't move the refrigerator while you're nine months pregnant. Keep the energy moving. When something starts to feel stagnant, something needs to change. Make subtle movements. Make grand-scale movements. Move off your chair and move your body in ways you never moved before. When nothing is moving and you are the cause, pick yourself up and move out of the way.

Music

Music has charms to soothe the savage beast, and it works pretty well on mothers and children, too. Whether jazz or hip-hop, country or bebop, music has the power to lift your spirits, file down the edges of a stressful day, and gently lull your four-year-old to sleep. Make your own kind of music and make beautiful music together. Play violin or play a pair of spoons. Rock out to the radio, or beat on makeshift drums made from pots, lids, and boxes. Introduce your child to the music of nature: the evening symphony of crickets, bullfrogs, and the plip-plop of stones skipped over a pond. Hear the drone of a low-flying plane, the whistle of the wind through a crack in the window, and the soft, gentle tinkle of wind chimes in a tree. The world is filled with music; make it your own.

Mystery

Some things just can't be explained. You don't know who did it, but it's done. You can't remember fixing it, but it's working. Yesterday the buds were tightly closed and today everything is blooming. You make the acquaintance of a brand-new being, and the next thing you know, you're in love. You tuck in a little girl with freckles on her nose, and when she wakes up, she's a young woman. How can you feel like a child yourself, yet know that you're really a mother? How can the world harbor so much joy and at the same time hold on to such sorrow? You feel like you can't go on another step, and somehow you summon the courage. You feel the presence of a son overseas, and just minutes later, he calls. A baby is born with her great-grandma's eyes, at the very moment the old woman passes. There's a wonder of life that you can't quite explain. It can only be labeled *mystery*.

Nature

You never outgrow your need for nature. There's a healing balm within a grove of trees, beside a trickling waterfall, woven into the wings of butterflies that can never be bought in a bottle. You can hide your thirst for wild, growing things and flamboyant sunrises and the fragrance of a sage-kissed meadow, but the thirst will only grow more demanding over time. If your life is too busy for intimacies with nature, then your life is far too busy to sustain—and much too hollow to pass with joy to your children. As often as you can, get as close to nature as you can. Take her senses up through your own and marry them in a most delicious dance. When you are askew and running in all directions, you can be sure what you need is nature. And you can be sure that you need it right now.

Needs

What's the use of having needs if you never dare to express them? You need some time alone, so you'd better come right out and ask for it. You need to get the back ready for planting, and you need everybody to help. If you need a tall person to bring down the holiday decorations from the top shelf, you'd better put your request in now. If you need some extra loving, don't expect others to read your mind; they might need a not-so-subtle hint. Need somebody to come in once a week for cleaning? Post a notice. Need to find the missing pieces to your favorite jigsaw puzzle? Sound the alert. Need more reservations for the seventh-grade dinner? You need to set up the phone tree, and now. Need a neck rub? Need a can of chili? Need a three-week vacation in Hawaii? Whatever you need, you might get it on eBay. But you need to state clearly your needs.

Neighbors

Who waters your plants when you go on vacation? Neighbors. Who called the fire department when the barn started smoking? Neighbors. Who threatened to sue when the boys rode their bikes through the Japanese pond? Neighbors. You see them over the fence or out by the mailbox, and sometimes never at all. They hear all of your yelling and hear the doors slamming and they bring you crates of zucchini when they've had enough. Their lemons fall on your lawn and your oranges drop onto theirs, so you decide to call it a draw. Their friends park in front of your driveway and leave cigarette butts on the curb, but at least their dog doesn't bark. Sometimes their children make your kids look lazy, but the blessing is they're not truly crazy. If you're lucky, you only have an occasional battle, but if I had my druthers, I'd live next to cattle.

News

New? Saundra got fired. The baby's got pneu-
monia. Lance lost first place at the wrestling
competition but still got his personal best. Alisha's
best friend is getting married in Scotland and all
of the men are going in kilts. The furnace went
out again at the cabin. The van won't be ready for
at least two more weeks. The biopsy was negative
but they're doing it over. It snowed two feet in
Buffalo but the temperature's climbing. Caroline's
pregnant. Patricia's not. Ellen went into labor this
morning and the doctor thinks it's triplets.
Edward passed in the night with a smile on his
lips. The cat's got diabetes and the lizard escaped
this past weekend. Amara's new puppy just gained
three pounds! They tore down the old drive-in
and are putting up a strip mall with a nail salon
and fish taco place. Ethan graduated at the top of
his class and his dad was so touched that he cried.
Call me if you hear any news.

Next!

You thought you found your perfect doctor, but you couldn't get an appointment for three and a half months. Next! It sounded like your dream apartment, but there was no parking for your Harley. Next! The agent acted like she was interested, but never returned your call. Next! The baby-sitter drank your best Napa wine and then hid the bottle in the hamper. Next! They treated you as though you didn't exist. Next! Her reputation was flawless, but her hairspray made you itch. Next! Promises were made, but too many were broken. Next! Your son was telling the truth, but the teacher refused to believe him. Next! Life's too short to spend time on situations that are hopelessly out of synch with your needs. If it isn't a *yes!* you can bet it's a *no.* Keep your options open. Next!

No

No, you can't stay out after midnight. No, you can't wash the ferret in the bathtub. Nope, no slumber parties on school nights. No way can you drive to the coast. No way are we getting another phone. No, sweetie, don't eat the marbles. No, honey, don't throw the night-light. No, there's no more ice cream and no, we're not going to get some. No, I can't iron your pants now. No, I can't be the basketball mom. No, I don't know where your shoes are. No, you can't go to Mexico for the weekend. Not while I'm working. Not until dinner. Not now, Daddy's sleeping. No, maybe later. How many times do I have to say no? No! Now don't ask me again! Yes, you can ask me to go out to dinner. Why on earth do you think I'd say no?

Nobody

You really can't argue with nobody. Who left the ice cream out until it melted into a puddle? Nobody. Who left the burner on most of the day? Nobody. Who does the ancient bagel (with cream cheese and ants) on the step belong to? Nobody. Nobody is the one for the job when it's dirty, smelly, or takes all day. Nobody knows anything at all about the broken dishes in the trash. Who can you depend on to baby-sit Saturday night? Nobody. Who took the charred chicken out of the oven when you got home late? Nobody. Who noticed that the toilet was overflowing and dripping down into the hallway? Nobody. Nobody is available when you need him (or her), but sometimes, nobody can be your best friend. Announce that you're headed out to a movie and ice cream and suddenly, everybody's asking who gets to go with you. What more perfect companion? Nobody.

Nostalgia

Ah, for the good old days! You and your girlfriends piled in the car and headed off without a care in the world. You lounged around for hours talking about who was the best dancer and who had the greatest behind. You'd sleep until noon every day if your mom would allow it. You left your hair in the sink and your homework on the sofa and only used the washer under duress. You baby-sat your little brother or sister if you had to, but you didn't do dishes or diapers. You were never shaken awake before dawn by a pair of warm, tiny hands or the kick of a foot in your side. You knew nothing of earaches or stomach flu or intolerable rashes unless they were your own. Never did you spend a full day with your baby in your arms, nestled close to your breast, depending on you for life itself. Funny how the good old days change.

Notes

There's a note from your doctor on the refrigerator, but it's buried so deep you never saw it and you missed the appointment that took three weeks to secure. The important note you left for the roofer was carried away by the wind. The note on the cooler says you only need a quart of skim this week, but you were late getting it out and the truck was already gone. There's a sticky note on the banister but your son threw his jacket over it and that's why the dinner's not thawed. Your kitchen counter is littered with notes for the day. The note that goes to the vet with the dog. The note asking day care to please remember sunscreen. You've got a note stuck to your bag to remind you to fill up the propane. A note taped to your visor so you won't forget the oil change. And here, under the newspaper, is the note your sweetie scribbled, saying "I love you so much." At least there's one noteworthy note.

Notice

It's hard not to notice. You get a glimpse of your teenager in the shower, and you notice the young woman she's become. Your son goes away for a week with his cousin, and when he comes back you notice the hair on his chin and the breadth of his shoulders. You walk by the bedroom at naptime and you notice your little one is pointing to letters and saying their names. You can't help but notice that the house seems more settled, that evenings are quieter when everyone's home. Kind of like walking by the same tree every day and suddenly noticing the buds and the leaves. You don't have to look so hard to notice that you've changed as a mother. You're growing by leaps and bounds just like your kids. It's impossible not to notice.

Nourish

With all the energy you spend feeding your children, remember to nourish yourself. Not only with grams and calories and protein and carbs, but with deeper nourishment that feeds you where you hunger most. Make sure your daily minimum requirements include large helpings of respect and multiple servings of acknowledgment. Not just for what you do every day, but simply for who you are. Replenish your inner supply of self-caring and worthiness at least three times every day. Make sure your place setting offers a tasty sampling of rest, relaxation, and solitude, balanced with generous spoonfuls of movement, exercise, deep breathing, and fun. Don't skimp on portions of personal expression: dance, sing, write, paint, sew, knit, build, cook. Top everything off by giving and receiving unconditional love by the bucketful, and season liberally by accepting yourself and others without judgment. Feed your spirit and feed your soul. Feel how true nourishment feels.

Now

No matter what the clock says, the only time is Now. That beautiful smile on your little one's face is Now, so don't miss it. The inquisitive eyes, the questions about love and babies, are happening Now, so don't put them off. Your teenager is asking your advice Now, and for all you know, it may be the first and last time it happens. This moment, with this child, on this day, will never come around again. So revel in the Now—and in every Now that's bound to follow. Focus your attention on this moment, this book, this child, this stormy night—not on what you're going to take to the dry cleaners tomorrow. Bring your presence to this scraped knee, to this picture of a pony, to this exquisite human connection right Now—not to a replay of the blowup you had yesterday with the man in accounting. Every time you retreat to the past or the future, you're certain to miss what is Now.

Offer

Make your life an offering. Offer to pay them for
the vegetables and if they look insulted,
remember not to offer again. Offer your hand to
a mother who needs one. Offer your kindness,
offer your heart's wisdom. Offer the spare room in
the basement if that's what she needs. When she
offers to help with yard work in return, graciously
agree to her offer. Make your daughter an offer
she can't refuse. Offer to buy her a car if she
offers to take you to Oregon. When the capital
campaign comes calling, offer whatever makes
you feel good inside. Receive their offer and offer
to look it over. Then make a counteroffer that
offers you more. Offer to work the concession
stand. Offer to drive to the state tournament, and
if gas money is offered, accept the offer with a
smile.

Open

Be open to miracles. Be open to the possibility that some things defy rational thought. It's not important whether you ultimately agree; what matters is that you remain open. Keep the discussion open until all the facts come in. Open your heart as well as your mind. Open your eyes and make your own observations. When it's wartime and your teenager talks about joining the service, be open even though you're afraid. When she talks about traveling for a year instead of going to college, be open to believing that this may be best for her. Be open to constructive criticism. **Open your ears and listen** to what others are saying. Trust enough to open up and share your deepest feelings. To open up so far that it feels uncomfortable. Even though you want to keep the door closed, you can't remain open and shut.

Opportunity

Opportunity abounds, wearing many guises. That mishap with the stove is your opportunity to focus yourself and pay greater attention. The brouhaha at the bank isn't a disaster; it's your chance to get a better handle on your financial affairs. Got some serious news from your doctor? Don't miss this opportunity to begin a healthier lifestyle. If you're given the opportunity to rise above a prickly situation, take it. What appears to be a loss of security is yet another opportunity to call up greater self-reliance. Do you feel conflict all around you? It may be your golden opportunity to grow into a fully realized human being. Opportunity lurks around corners and waits for you under the stairs where you can too easily avoid it. Set your intention to hear the call of opportunity. When opportunity comes knocking, get out of the shower and answer the door.

Oracles

Signs are everywhere if you take time to look. You're wondering what musical to revive at the high school, and a copy of *Grease* falls off the video store shelf. You're frazzled and fried with an overloaded schedule and two days later, your circuit breakers blow. You run out of gas on the way to the chiropractor, who later informs you your adrenal glands are shot. For all the times you've asked for a sign, have you paid attention and noticed the answer? You can't make up your mind about getting your tubes tied, and the answer comes back that you're pregnant. You feel like you're drowning and the washer floods to confirm your suspicions. Your job is making you sick and you know you can't take it, and lo and behold, here come layoffs! Oracles show up in the most ordinary places. Take your blinders off and the signs will appear.

Order

You don't need to be a neatnik to appreciate order.
There's something comforting about waking up
and walking into a clean kitchen. Somehow the
day gets off to a better start when you don't begin
by facing a sink full of cold, greasy dishes. When
you can enter the house without tripping over in-
line skates, backpacks, jackets, and old lunches,
you can breathe out and move on with the next
order of business. The high point of the day is
finding your toothbrush exactly where you left it.
And it's still clean! Bringing order to toys and
books is child's play. Sort and pile and organize
and separate like objects and colors into baskets.
Your work flows more smoothly when you work
in an orderly setting. An orderly mind leads to
orderly work. Order is more than fanatical
cleaning. When there's order in the house, you
create order in your soul.

Originality

If there's a book on standard operating procedures for mothers, pretend you never heard of it. If someone has compiled a list of what's hot and what's not in mothering this year, be sure to avoid it. Be your own unique article! Turn heads with your one-of-a-kind ways. Somebody has to be the mom who paints her fingernails six different shades, so why not you? Someone's school lunch is bound to contain escargot and jelly on matzo, so why not your child's? While all the other moms are scout leaders and soccer coaches, only you can be the one who plays sax in biker bars on weekends. Who says you can't bring brie to the sixth-grade bake sale—or your collection of four-inch spike heels to the church bazaar? No state in the union has declared originality a crime, but stifling your style in the name of motherhood can keep your spirit locked up for a lifetime.

Outlets

This is not about shopping for discount dinner-
ware. This is about finding safe, enjoyable chan-
nels for all your creative energy. The job of
mothering may be full time and a half, yet it
won't satisfy all of your urges. If you need an
outlet where you can blow off steam, join a gym
and power-step your way to serenity. Get yourself
to an African drumming circle and breathe to the
rhythm of the beat. When you feel starved for
intellectual stimulation, go to college lectures and
bookstore signings and hook up with others to
exercise your brain. Wanting to do more with
your fingers than paint? Sign up for a pottery
class, for a jewelry-making workshop, for piano
lessons. Finding it hard to give up babies as your
children grow? Volunteer at a hospital where you
can rock tiny infants to sleep. It's sound energy
policy to plug into an outlet. The danger is
blowing your fuse if you don't.

Overlook

Granted, some things you can't ignore. The stakes
are too high. The issues too important. The
outcome far too monumental. In between, there
are lots and lots of opportunities to overlook.
Mothers need to choose their battles wisely. Your
teenager has an excellent record for getting home
on time, so you can overlook that recent trans-
gression. Usually the bathroom is kept pretty
clean, so that mess Saturday morning, you can
just overlook. Your respectful daughter hurled
some harsh insults your way, but just this one
time, you can waive it. Overlook that little incident with the hair dryer without making a federal
case of it. That tiff over the spilled cup of tea?
Never happened. That old scarf that somehow got
used for a brake job? It really didn't matter, so
what's the big deal? Don't let the details get under
your skin. Keep the peace and choose to
overlook it.

Partner

Mothering as a singleton is a long and lonely road. Partners can make all the difference. Find a partner who's committed to helping you raise your children, if that's what you want. Find a partner who's committed to you for yourself. Locate a group of baby-sitting partners and start your own co-op. Find a golf partner. A tennis partner. A dance partner who knows how to lead as well as follow. Hook up with some play partners for your child; all the better if the moms can play, too. Partner up to bake and cook a month of meals in advance. Then get together as dining partners and eat them. Find a business partner who can co-create a vision and help bring it to life. Form a partnership if you wish. Bridge partner? Poker partner? Theater partner? Buddy? It's all much more fun when you share life with partners.

Passion

The greatest gift that you have is your passion.
It gives rise to children and art and radical new
ideas and fiery politics and the seeds that lead to
creation. Pure passion has no equal in power. It
fuels change and builds communities and cracks
open hearts with its potency. Passion is your
companion when you're holding two jobs and
selling your jewelry so your babies can go on to
college. It's passion that transforms the old gas
station into a health center and brings harmony
into a city divided. Unleash your passion and you
rock the world. Whether you mother, manage, or
manufacture, infuse it with passion. If your
passion is painting, poetry, piano, or peace, make
your mark. When you're on fire for love, that's
passion. When spirit moves through your body,
that's passion. When you connect with your
passion, nothing can stop you. A life with no
passion is no life at all.

Pasta

What would moms do without noodles? Spirals and macaroni and noodles in the shape of letters and numbers and stars and stripes. What else can be served seven times a week without ever seeming stale? What other dinner item can be painted and strung into necklaces and glued into mosaics and turned into musical rattles and rain sticks and multicultural holiday decorations? Drench pasta with cheese and presto! It's lunch for the hungry hordes! Spray them with gold paint and glitter to make magnificent gilded pencil cups and napkin holders, and your gift-giving list is complete. Even better—noodles are as entertaining as they are tasty! They make perfect pucks for tabletop hockey and have filled in as moustaches, eyebrows, and all manner of bugs. Who needs videos when you have vermicelli? Boil up the water and get out the napkins! We're nibbling on noodles again!

Patience

Be patient with children, for they have so much to learn. Be patient with yourself for the very same reason. Slow down and give everyone a chance to breathe. Let time breathe. Let space breathe. Be patient enough to let a situation sort itself out—and be willing to wait for a surprising solution. Patience asks you to let go of your need for the quick fix. Patience asks you to sit back longer than feels comfortable and let time work its wonder. It might take minutes; it may take days. If you allow, patience will lead you past your old, tired, either-or approach to mothering and into a new world of possibilities. With patience on your side you can respond more and react less. You can hear what questions are truly being asked, because you're not so busy blurting out instant answers. There's no magic formula for patience. You simply rein in the impulse to jump forward, and create a moment for patience to step in. Then give a little of your time to patience.

Pause

Before you go on, take a moment. Pause. Give
yourself some time and space to breathe. Pause.
Everybody's starving for dinner. Pause. The tele-
phone is ringing. Pause. Before you go on, take a
moment. Pause. They're all waiting for your
answer. Pause. They want you to do it right now.
Pause. You're rushing your daughter through
breakfast. Pause. It's time you got out the door.
Pause. Before you go on, take a moment. Pause.
The dryer is buzzing. Pause. The oven is beeping.
Pause. The teakettle's whistling. Pause. The twins
are calling. Pause. Before you go on, take a
moment. Pause. Someone's knocking at the back
door. Pause. The show's almost starting. Pause.

You're losing your patience.

Pause.

Give yourself some time and space to breathe.

Pause.

Before you go on, take a moment to pause.

Peace

Peace becomes a mother. An unmistakable artistry
lives within a peaceful scene of mother and child.
They may be inside or outside, dressed in finery
or barely dressed at all. They might be sleeping
together like spoons or sitting and rocking, with
serenity written all over their lovely faces and a
hint of halos above their heads. Babes in arms,
babes at the breast, wrapped tightly against a
familiar heartbeat, sacked out peacefully under
the shade of a willow tree. Time stands motion-
less when peace is in the air and on the breath of
a mother. Find peace for yourself whenever you
can and you create peace for all time. Learn to
create peace within, when you're surrounded by
nothing peaceful at all. Peace has a quality all its
own, much larger than the absence of war. When
mothers are at peace, the world has a chance.
When children learn peace, they will teach it all
their lives.

Peer

Sit by a clear-running stream and peer at your own reflection. Try to see past your masks and through your illusions. Who is that lurking inside? Peer deeply into the eyes of another and see how far you can see within. Can you cross through the gateway to soul? When an infant peers at you wide-eyed as if to say "What's going on in there?" peer back with the same intention. Peer into darkened doorways before you make an entrance. Peer around corners and into the trunks of trees, and try not to scream if you see eyes peering back. Peer through a microscope and marvel at the dance of your own cellular makeup. Peer through a telescope and come eye-to-eye with the moon. Could it be that he's winking? Maybe yes, maybe no. Things are not always how they appear.

Photos

Here's the baby in his stroller. Here's his sister on
her bike. Here's the day we all went fishing. Here's
the gang with Uncle Mike. Here's my nephew at
bar mitzvah. Here's that weekend at the lake.
Here's Mom and Dad—we caught them kissing.
Oh, look at the birthday girl eating her cake!
Here's a shot of graduation. Here's another and
three more. Here's our trip to San Diego. Here's a
great shot of our kitchen door. Here's the bride-
groom. There's the ring. There's that woman they
hired to sing. Here's the baby dolled up for Easter.
Here's a shot of the marshmallow eggs. Check out
this photo of your Grandma Esther. Now you
know where you got those legs! Here's a shot at
the beach in August. Here's the lodge where we
went to ski. Do you have just one more minute?
I have a few pictures I want you to see.

Plans

My mother lived for her plans. She wrote them on
napkins and stuck them on the mirror in the
bathroom where she reviewed them every day.
She planned a trip to Africa. She planned to go to
law school after all the kids were grown. She had
a plan for amassing a million dollars by the time
she was forty. In between her more grandiose
plans, she planned out which variety of beans to
plant in her garden, and where. During the
winter, the refrigerator door was plastered with
plans for the holidays. Who would come. What
we would eat. A plan for doing presents. You
could see my mother scribbling on a tiny notebook she wore on a ribbon around her neck.
Jotting down notes for her plans. She never went
to Africa, though. Never got to law school. Her
garden had peppers, but I don't remember beans.
Her plans kept her going, but they never went far.
That's one of the problems with plans.

Play

When baby's finished sleeping and all done eating, it's playtime! So find yourself a shady spot under a big umbrella, and start digging your way to China. Bubble up the bathtub and poof! you're a submarine. Let Daddy play toss-and-tumble and Mom play soft-and-gentle, and then trade places and double everyone's fun! Toys and games are where you find them. Turn your kitchen into a wonderland of wooden spoons, plastic containers, and skyscrapers made one can at a time. Get down on all fours and crawl into a magic kingdom of cushions and sheets and billowy scarves. Who's that choo-choo doing the cha-cha? Who's that bronco rarin' to buck? The only rules of play are these: stay safe, giggle all you want, and keep at it till everybody's played out. Then plop on the pillows like napping puppies—until you're ready to wake up and play it again.

Pockets

This one's got tissues and hair ties and a piece of
a comb. Over here are the pencils, some wipes,
and what appears to be a peach pit of unknown
origin. You've got a dime and three pennies in this
one, kind of sticky from the lip-gloss that went in
without its lid. In your back pocket you've got a
twenty-dollar bill and your just-in-case credit
card. This big one used to carry the key to the
bike lock, the phone number of a babysitter new
in town, and a ketchup packet from the drive-
through. Now all that's in it is a hole. You put the
insect repellent back here before, but *ouch!* it
seems to have wandered. Even though you put the
note to the principal in your daughter's shirt
pocket and buttoned it tight, somehow it never
arrived. You were thrilled to get a postcard from
the folks on the road, but where did you pocket
your glasses?

Popcorn

Let's pop the question for popcorn! Was there
ever invented a more perfect snack? Popcorn turns
TV into a night at the movies and stands in as
dinner when you can hardly stand. Drenched in
salt and butter, drizzled with olive oil and herbs,
or smothered in melted brown sugar and butter,
popcorn hits the spot every time. And it sells for
practically peanuts! It satisfies slumber parties and
Halloween get-togethers, and decorates quite
nicely your holiday tree. Don't tell them it's really
just bird food. Bring it out in pots and bowls and
pop it by the pound. When the freezer is empty
and the chips are all gone, what a treat to fall
back into popcorn! The lunchmeat is finished?
Not a single piece of bread? Go ahead, Mom, just
reach for the popcorn.

Porches

When you can't quite stay in and you can't quite go out, porches are utterly perfect. Screened-in porches for late summer board games and strawberry shortcake and books scattered over the painted wooden floor. Back porches where you can barbecue in the rain and finger-paint on the old kitchen table and wash hands in the faucet outdoors. Porches with antique rocking chairs and brand-new chaise lounges for napping when inside the beds are perfectly made. Porches don't have to be fancy; they just have to be porches. Two steps and a concrete pad sized right for quiet conversation. Decks where you can tend your prized petunias without having to put on your shoes. Tiny porches with just enough room for a toddler, a Popsicle, and a song about picnics. There's a warm, fuzzy feeling that you've gone far away when you plant yourself out on the porch.

Possibility

There is no end to possibility. It encompasses everything you could ever think of, plus a vast universe beyond the reaches of your mind. When you feel your possibilities shrinking, it's only because you've stopped looking, not because they've disappeared. Being a mother doesn't thwart your range of possibilities—it invites you to expand your horizons. If it's not possible to work full-time right now, you can work part-time. If it's impossible to return to your old company, you can create new professional relationships with others. If your chosen career doesn't seem aligned with your mothering, choose again. Don't convince yourself or others that it's impossible. Between your old ideas of this or that lie hundreds of possibilities. Are you open to creating a model that's never existed before? Can you entertain an idea that is wildly outside the bounds of anything you've ever tried? You can, when you believe in possibility.

Potluck

Hands down, one of the finest ideas ever created
for mothers! Tables filled with delectable main
dishes, savory soups and salads, veggies deluxe,
desserts galore. All made by someone else! Plenty
of bread and butter, chips and salsa, carrots and
celery, and cheese and fruit by the platter. All
prepared by someone else! A potluck is a
Hawaiian vacation, pennies from heaven, a
winning lottery ticket. Potlucks mean no pots to
wash (unless you're bringing pasta), no dishes to
dry, and best of all, no incessant debates over
what's for dinner. Jamie gets gelatin salad, Jim gets
teriyaki chicken, spaghetti for Shakena, and for
Mom (Could it be?) salmon salad. Nearly any
lecture, almost any slide show, practically every
program you can imagine, is worth it if preceded
by potluck. Grab the kids and head for the drive-
through—then straight to the Jordans for potluck!

Prayer

Embrace prayer. It doesn't matter how you do it,
or where you do it, or what you call it when you
do. All that matters is that you open yourself up
to a conversation with someone or something
larger and grander than you. You can hear yourself speak the words or come forth silently with
prayer in your heart. You can find your prayers in
books and on the walls of churches and
synagogues and mosques, or you can let prayer be
born in the moment you surrender to prayer.
Choose a language. Choose a faith tradition.
Choose simply to talk with a dear and trusted
friend who is wiser and richer and more experienced than you. Admit you're confused. Admit
you're tired. Ask for help and guidance and the
power of love to heal. Give thanks for all that you
have and all that you don't and know that it all is
enough. The busiest mother has got to believe
that it's worth it to take time for prayer.

Priorities

Why is it so hard to honor what's truly important in your life? Priorities don't need to be set as much as they need to be acknowledged. Your health matters more than your paycheck, right? Your family's well-being is a higher priority than a new car, yes? Your commitment to your God, your spirit, or your soul is a higher commitment than any business agreement you may have entered, is it not? Living your life authentically takes precedent over following the latest media-driven trends, doesn't it? Be clear about the three or four things that are at the top of your list. Your own well-being. Your children's well-being. Your marriage. Your spiritual relationships. Your community. Your planet. Your service to humanity. Once you are crystal clear about your priorities, it's easy to weed out anything that doesn't support them. And even easier to value everything that does. Your top priority is to know what matters most to you. And your next is to act from that knowing.

Privacy

Admit it. You need some privacy—and what's more, you deserve it big time! More than those few blissful minutes in the bathroom with the door locked. More than those stolen moments waiting for red lights to change or driving through the car wash. You need drawers that others can't get into and clothes that are yours and yours alone. A shelf to hold your treasures and keep them out of harm's way. And yes, a room to call your own. A space where you can think without interruption and talk to your mate without whispering like thieves in the night. Where you can wear what you want, as little as you want, and be alone for whatever you need. Without begging. Without blowing up and slamming doors. Without asking anyone for permission. There's no big secret to privacy. Just name it and claim it as yours.

Promise

When it comes to promises, a mother always
stands her ground. When she promises you can
call if the party turns ugly, no matter what time it
is, she'll be there. When she gives her word to
keep you in the school you love, you'd better
believe she'll move hell and high water to make
good on her promise. Cross my heart and hope to
die; stick a needle in my eye. It's a promise. Moms
need to keep the promises they make to themselves, too. Promise to take exceedingly good care
of yourself. Promise to tend to your marriage
even as a houseful of kids threatens to overrun it.
Promise to keep enough of yourself in the face of
your limitless giving. Promise? When you look in
the eyes of a child that you love, you know you
could never back down on a promise. Promise to
look long and hard at yourself and equally honor
your promise.

Prosper

Live well and prosper. Create a life of abundance and leave lack and scarcity by the side of the road. Remember that money is one currency, yet it's not the only one. What is the state of your balance sheet? One mother prospers materially, yet aches for more time with her toddler. Her pockets are deep, yet she feels a deficit in her heart. Another offers the riches of spirit and prayer, trust and faith, yet can't buy the latest clothes or toys. For some it's a question of cash. For others, the issue is flow. Find your point of prosperity in all things. Enlarge your picture of success to include time, space, freedom, joy, and love. If the sum total leaves you feeling prosperous, you are. If you sense something's missing, it probably is. Bottom line? Your net worth is no measure of your value as a mother. You're as young and as rich as you feel.

Protect

Protecting your child behind locked doors and walls of fear is no protection at all. Teaching a child that danger lurks around every corner, that terror lives in every heart, inflicts an inner violence all its own. The greatest protection in an unsettled world is to protect yourself from thoughts of fear. Shield yourself and your child from blaring media reports and a constant diet of war, mayhem, and injustice. Just don't go there! Think of changing the channel of your life, and surround yourself with a reality in which no harm threatens and all is well. Know that you are protected from fear and want, scarcity and lack, by something grander and gloriously created in love. Inside every mother is an endless river of protection more powerful than deadbolts and alarms and fingers clenched in fear. When you stop rushing to provide every ounce of protection, you'll rest in the knowledge that all is secure.

Proud

A mother's pride wells up from her heart, never arrogant nor boastful. It's the feeling you get when your child leaves the party as soon as the drinking begins. It's watching your baby make her way across the stage after they told you she'd never walk again. How proud can one mother be? Yours was the child who stood up to protect the one being threatened. Yours was the child who stood firm with the truth. Yours was the boy who just said no, when everyone else said, "Whatever." She's the first to finish college, and the entire family is proud. He spends his weekends helping elders, and it makes you feel so proud. He wasn't the smartest, the fastest, or the best, but he held his head high and you've always been proud. You raised them up well, they're fine human beings. You have every right to be proud.

Pursue

Whatever you desire most, go after it. Pursue your dreams like a relentless hunter going after its prey. Keep your intention clear and move closer to your target with laser-sharp precision. Pursue your college degree—no matter how long you've been away from school. Pursue your dream of owning your own silkscreen studio or your own café. Pursue what's best for your child. Check out websites, read all you can, and go for the gold. Pursue the truth. Peel back the layers and the confusion and aim straight for the heart of the matter. Leave no stone unturned in your quest for authenticity. Take on a goal and persevere onward through the fog. Follow the light at the end of the tunnel and know that it's more than a freight train coming at you. Continue in hot pursuit of your dreams, and nothing can stand in your way.

Push

One last push and you're done! Push yourself a little more and it's over. Breathe out so you don't have to push quite so hard. Release and let the push come from within. Once in a while, you can push yourself to the limit, but remember next time to pull back. With one graceful push, you're over the top and coming down the other side. Ask someone to give you a boost, to push you enough to get going. It doesn't have to be a kick in the butt; a sweet little pat will do fine. Don't apologize for being pushy. It's a pushy mother who can get the job done. Push gently so others don't push back too hard. (They don't like you pushing their buttons!) If your children even think about pushing you around, let them know they've pushed way too far. If pushing gets you nowhere, pull some strings.

Questions

Where did I come from? Who do you love most?
When will we get there? Are we close to a bathroom? Can I have a cookie? Is there any more pie?
Who took the last piece of pizza? Do I look fat to
you? Do you like my hair? Do you mean it? What
is that thing that you're wearing? How can you go
out in public like that? Who told you you could
get a nose ring? Have you seen my keys? Did you
borrow my razor? Are those your magazines down
behind the furnace? Do you know how handsome
you look in black? Do you know how great you
look in white? Can I have five dollars? Can I have
ten dollars? Could you loan me twenty bucks
until Tuesday? What would you ever do without
me? What would I do without you? Do you know
how much I love you? Does anyone know where
the remote is? Can you ever stop asking these
questions?

Rain

Rain, rain, come to stay. Have yourself a rainy day! Listen to the pitter of the rain on the roof and the patter of rain on the windows. Make it a day for gingerbread women and men, and chamomile tea with honey. The rain wants you to snuggle in bed a bit longer. The clouds want nothing more than to damp down your day. Bring out the paper and paints and puzzles and finger-paint pictures of rain. The rhythm of the rain is a respite. Pull on boots and bright slickers to enter the rain. Stomp in puddles and let the rain soak the hair peeking out of your rain hat. Walk alone in the rain, blessing each drop for the life it sustains. Feel the rain rolling down the back of your neck and dripping off your fingers. Wait up for the rainbow that follows the rain.

Raise

Raising children is two parts art, one part science, and at least three parts luck. Raise your children to be kind and you've won half the battle. Raise them to be loving, and they're well on their way. Lift them up out of selfishness and prejudice and you've raised human beings who can create a bright future. To raise a child who knows who he is, show him who you are. To raise a child who can carve out the life she is meant to live, hand her the sword of truth and clarity. The child who understands that life is an adventure and not an end goal has observed you living the same way. The child who knows the value of asking questions and needing no answers has been raised to thrive in a fast-changing world. Raise your child's awareness of the interconnection of all things. Raise her to understand that she will discover a rich life when her heartfelt words are followed by committed actions. With that kind of upbringing, your child will never fall.

Ready

No one is ever really ready to be a mother. You can read the books and watch the videos and take all kinds of classes, but, like winter, it will still knock you off your feet like a bolt out of the blue. You can get the nursery ready, get the tiny clothes ready, and ready yourself with all kinds of gear. You can be all ready with a car seat and a rocker and diapers galore. No matter what you do to prepare, don't be surprised if you still don't feel ready. How do you ready yourself for this new creature who's been living inside your body? How can you possibly anticipate the emotions that will grab you and shake you and transform you to the core? How can you feel ready for something you've only experienced from afar? Think about it like this: as soon as you get that you'll never be ready, the baby will say, "Ready or not, here I come!"

Reality

Stop living in someone else's and create your own. If your reality includes homeschooling, fresh-baked bread every morning, and a horse out back, you'll never be happy at a desk job in the city. So don't even try! If you're at home with fine Napa wine, designer clothes, Sunday at the symphony, and a nanny trained in Europe's best tradition, then your reality probably won't include tubing with the kids down by Muddy Creek. When someone demands that you face reality, your first question should be "Which one?" You build your own reality on thoughts, words, and actions that line up with your personal worldview. One mother sees a world filled with love, light, and the blessings of angels; another feels beset by the terror of war and impending doom. Who can judge which is truly reality? Only the mother who makes it her own.

Receive

Offer someone the gift of giving to you. For once, let yourself be the one who receives. Receive a gift of helping hands, of food, of money, of love, of recognition. Sit back and accept a gift of tender loving care. Don't argue, don't refuse, don't make excuses. Receive graciously and with gratitude. If you've always been a giver, now is the time for you to receive. Voice what you need. A tricycle? Clothing? Connections? A friend? Let down your defenses and your tough-gal exterior. Prepare to receive all that you deserve and know that it will be provided. Let go of your white-knuckled, stressed-out grasp on life and let your palms fill with overflowing abundance. Someone wants to help you receive. Drop your foolish pride and tell him or her you're willing. Willing and ready to receive.

Reclaim

Unearth parts of yourself that are buried away, and reclaim the totality of who you are. Reclaim your music, your writing, your handwork. Recover your spontaneity, the free-spiritedness that once all but defined you. Reclaim that overgrown plot of ground and create a meditation garden. Reclaim that old sandstone building on Main Street, and uncover the businesswoman inside you. If you feel you've lost some essential ingredient along the way, go back and pick it up again. Reclaim two quiet hours each day. Reclaim your self-respect. Reclaim your faith in your God, no matter who has tried to wrest it away. Backtrack until you rediscover the jewels you once stepped over and the tangled stories that have tripped you up. Recover your health and emotional wellness. Name it and reclaim it, and you know that it's yours.

Recognize

Recognize that you do not own your children.
They are not yours to keep, simply to watch over
and guide through this phase of their lives.
Recognize that you are but one infinitesimal part
of a glorious whole, and that every mother is you
and every child is yours, as well. How then can
you set yourself apart, feeling that your trials and
your joys are yours alone? How can you claim that
no others understand you, that none can relate to
your fears and doubts or ever offer comfort
worthy of your pain? When you recognize that
you are not an island to yourself, you will drop
your top-heavy sense of self-reliance and let
others catch you when you fall. When you have
the insight that opens you to deeper knowing,
you will move as a mother who is mothered
by all.

Reconsider

Don't be so tied to your thoughts that you can't think again. Revisit the situation with a different perspective and try to see things in a new light. Replay the movie in your mind and discover details you didn't notice before. If your zero tolerance for piercing has left your teenager in tears, reconsider. Run through the pros and cons again. Ask a few more questions and listen with new ears to the answers. Review your actions and reconsider whether you might have done things differently. Maybe you acted hastily. Perhaps your words were overly aggressive. Could it be that you were not nearly as open-minded as you believed yourself to be? Reconsidering doesn't mean admitting you were wrong the first time: it means you are open to new information and changing dynamics. Mothers aren't always right and their children aren't always wrong. The least you can do is reconsider.

Redefine

If language is alive, why not redefine it? Redefine perfection and know that you've attained it. Redefine success in your own terms and know that it's yours. If you cringe when people talk about wealth, redefine currency and riches in the way that you see them. If you don't agree with society's definition of religion, come up with one of your own. A lot of people toss around the idea of family values; maybe we should just redefine them. There's a lot of focus on spirit and angels; why not just define them as love? Redefine yourself as a lightworker—if that's what you really do. Redefine yourself as a goddess, if that's who you truly are. Birth mother? Foster mother? Adoptive mother? Stepmother? Why not simplify the whole thing and call it what you are? A mother's a mother's a mother.

Reflect

Before you act, reflect. Take time to ponder without any need to figure things out or come to a quick solution. Give yourself time to reflect on that sticky incident. Can you now see a different perspective? Do you have a deeper understanding of what really went on? Are you feeling greater compassion for the others involved? Consider whether you could have created a different scenario with your son's teacher. Allow that you might have approached the coach from a different place. Perhaps you could tread a bit more lightly the next time the baby pulls every can out of the cupboard and every label off of every can. Give yourself just ten minutes to reflect, and more when you are able. Don't judge your actions, just look at them again, like a snow globe you turn over and over in your hand, until you see clearly what was hidden before. Don't rush to repair. Just reflect.

Refuge

There must be a place where you can let down your guard. Where there's no one to look after and no responsibilities to shoulder, where for a few blessed moments you don't need to watch your back. Take refuge where you can find it. Miles away from anything or in the sixth row of seats on the bus. Sitting quietly while you wait for your appointment. Surrounded by silence or within an envelope of serenity you create from within. Safe and protected from the forces that pull at your well-being without invitation. Practice taking refuge. Close your eyes and drift—without the expectation of being yanked back by a cough in the darkness. Soften your ears below the noise, taking refuge in a rich, dark silence. Taking heart that someone else will hear the phone, the door, the buzzer declaring the dryer is done. When you're feeling endangered, seek refuge.

Refuse

Just say no. Refuse to be pushed around by people or policies that are not in your best interest. Refuse to subject your child to unnecessary procedures—even if everyone else does it. Refuse to be pigeonholed or labeled or shoved into convenient boxes, and make sure the same goes for your children. Refuse gifts that aren't really gifts at all. Never place your family in situations where they may not be safe. And when others tell you you're overreacting, simply refuse to listen. When the offer of support comes with a long list of conditions, politely refuse. If their job requires you to put your principles on hold for the sake of their profits, walk away and don't look back. Refuse to be swept along by fear and judgment. Refuse to participate in activities that exclude others on account of whatever. When anything feels that it just can't be right, say, "No. Not this time. I refuse."

Release

Let go of anything that ties you up or holds you
down. Like apron strings that hold your children
too close for too long. Let go of those suitcases
and backpacks crammed full of old hurts,
unhealed wounds, unspoken words, unlived
moments, and unfulfilled dreams. Just loosen your
grasp and watch them float off into a shimmering
sky. Release yourself from the walls that you've
built between you and others, between you and
yourself. The walls you created to protect your
tender heart, fragile soul. Make a list of others'
rules and shoulds and have-tos, then tear up the
list and write your own! Release any fears. The
fear of being the wrong kind of mother, the fear
of losing control, the fear of judgment, ridicule,
or scorn. Release any fears and replace them now
with love. Hold aloft a bouquet of feathery
dandelions and release them to the wind. See how
easily they scatter in all directions when you
loosen your grip. When you loosen your grip and
let go.

Remember

Remember what it means to be a child, and what it means to be a mother. Remember the very best of what you were taught by your mother or your grandmother or by anyone who loved you well. If it hurts too much to remember, then forget. Look back through old pictures. Remember when you all piled into the car and drove far away from the city and swam and played all summer? Remember that birthday party when the dog got to the cake before you and your friends did? Remember what it feels like to be so small, and remember to laugh and to cry. And if sometimes you feel as if you remember nothing at all, remember this: your child may remember for a lifetime what you give to that child today.

Resources

When you're feeling less than abundant, take stock of your resources. You can include the financial variety, but that's only the beginning. Fort Knox would never hold all your resources. Your experiences. Your knowledge. Your constitution. Your health. Your skills. Your talents. Your temperament. Add in the people who care about you and would drop everything to come to your aid. Don't forget your faith, your trust, your belief in the infinite goodness of people. You've got resources you acquired while you were just a kid and you're still profiting from them today. Your stubborn will. Your attention to detail. The colorful history you received from past generations—and the living legacy you'll sign over to the next. Even in times when your portfolio plummets, your resource reserves remain strong. Your rich store of assets goes far beyond money, and it still barely touches your worth.

Retrieve

Go and get it! Dive in headfirst and swim farther than you ever swam before, and bring back what you've missed for so long. Return to your child-hood home and pick up the long-forgotten memories. The ones buried under the others. Pick up the last box that sits dusty in the attic and pick up the treasures still lying inside. Grab on to that elusive chunk of your history and this time, don't let it go. Parts of you lie littering the landscape, and it's time that you retrieved them. Get back your spirit. Your joie de vivre. Your captivating smile. Go back and get everything you left on the shelf. Hold it tight between your teeth. Hold it pressed to your heart. You lost it before.

Don't lose it again.

Reverence

Find something sacred in each and every day. Carve out a tiny piece of time when you think of nothing else but the sanctity of existence. Or don't even think at all. Simply sit. Listen. Pray. Feel the beating of your heart and the dance of your breath. Heed the magnificence of the now in its immeasurable glory. Reverence won't fight its way into your life. It won't come bursting through in a spare moment between calling the electrician and complaining about the taste of the ham. Any time you hear a hush or observe a bee hopping from flower to flower or feel the flutter of a newborn's eyelashes, reverence is there. If you are fortunate enough to witness a birth in the wild. If you are gifted with the opportunity to lay down the first footprints in a field of fresh-fallen snow. If you but stop and look and listen within, you will find yourself wrapped up in reverence.

Rhythm

Never try to dance to someone else's rhythm.
You'll trip over your feet and fall on your face and
nothing will feel like it fits. Follow your own
rhythms, your own tempo, and you're as graceful
as a willow in the wind. Move in rhythm to the
seasons, going inward when winter calls you, and
preparing soil and planting seeds when you feel
the stirrings of spring. Come to know the
rhythms of the moon, and utilize the energy in
each cycle as you start new projects, breathe life
into their bones, and carry them to their fullest
brilliance and inevitable completion. Follow the
rhythm of your body's cycles. Morning people are
mismatched when they work into darkness; night
owls never function well in the dawn's early light.
When you create a household, be sure to consider
its rhythm. Give everyone space to discover his or
her heartbeat, then drum up a rhythm where all
beat as one.

Right

Heart-centered well-being isn't about being right or wrong. It's not a question of always knowing the right answers. It's never about your ego's need to be the one who is right. Rightfulness leads you to principles that are just and fair. What's right is born from good and creates greater goodness. When it's right, you know it. You do the right thing at the right time in the right manner. You feel the rightness in your belly, calm and quiet. You feel a quickening in your body if rightness is a new place for you to be. Right relationship calls you to honor and value every child and every adult. When you are in line with right livelihood, your work instills you with a brilliance that expands through the universe and fosters no harm. It is right to consider the consequences of your actions on your own and future generations. It is right to teach your children to feel the difference in what is right.

Rise

Rise before the dawn, before the kids, before the day takes on its bright and brilliant intensity. Rise quietly and hear the morning bird song. Rise slowly, giving thanks for a new day unlike any other. Rise in silence so you have a better chance at rising above the chaos and the din that the day will surely bring. Pick yourself up by the scruff of your own neck and rise above anything or anyone that wants to pull you down. Rise above jealousy. Rise above ego. Always, always, rise above fear. Rise up and show everyone around you that there is a higher road. That kindness matters. That in the end, love conquers all. Make sure your children see you rise. Later you can nap. Later you can fall into a heap. But now, while the day is sweet and fresh and new, do yourself a favor and rise.

Rock

You are one rockin' mama! You're rocking that baby to sleep, softly crooning lullabies your great-grandma brought over from the Old Country. You're rocking back and forth in the checkout line at the grocery, arms wrapped around a twenty-five-pound bag of cat food like it was your firstborn. You're rocking the boat at work and making waves at City Hall, inciting others to do the right thing for mothers and their children. When everybody's off to school, you're rocking out to classic rock 'n' roll. You're groovin' and movin' and workin' up a powerful sweat and it feels so good! You rock! The car radio's blaring and the carpool is rocking to the seat-belt, hip-hop boogie. You're rocking and stomping at the town picnic, and women half your age are trying to get down and keep up. Rock-a-bye baby in the tree-tops, when the wind blows, Momma's gonna rock!

Roll

Sometimes you're so buy pushing the stone up the mountain, that you forget how easily it can roll down the other side. You lose sight of the power of momentum and keep gunning yourself in high gear long after gravity starts doing its job. It's no mystery why the tough times feel rocky and the good times roll. If you can roll with the punches, you can go with the flow. See your life path as an endless series of peaks and valleys. Sometimes you're struggling to gain ground, and other times momentum carries you along. When you're on a roll, you set yourself on autopilot and cruise. Get down with your child and do a forward tumble. Push yourself off and see how it feels to somersault down a grassy incline. Once you get in gear, there's nothing to do except roll.

Romance

Give yourself a chance for romance. Bundle the kids over to Judy's house, chill a good bottle of wine, and turn the lights down low. Yes, you still adore roses! Of course, you enjoy dressing up for dinner out and a light romantic movie. Moonlight walks and a twilight sail still make you shiver. Invite romance in with a provocative letter sprayed with provocative perfume. Leave a romantic message where the object of your affection is sure to find it. Rendezvous on the front porch or the back deck when the rest of the house is asleep. Light your way with romantic candles, lacy cover-ups, and the glow of your smile. Share romantic poetry against a backdrop of the most romantic music. Impossible, you say? At the very least, curl up with a romance novel that will spice up the night after bath time. Rent the most romantic movie you've ever seen, and slip into your most romantic sleepwear. It's a surefire cure for an incurable romantic.

Rules

No running. No playing. No children. No pets. Who wrote these rules? No bare feet. No bare midriff. No bare shoulders. Who wrote these rules? Now that you're the mom, you get to make the rules, then break the rules, then make them again. Who wrote these rules? You did. Who gets to enforce them? You do. So create some good ones. Like moms shower first—and last if they want. He who leaves the toilet seat up scrubs the bathtub. And she who hasn't finished her home-work pays $1.10 a minute to talk on the phone. Who ever laid down the law that beds have to be made as soon you get up? (As if!) Who decreed that a mother gives up the last brownie to a whimpering child? You can wipe the slate clean of rules that repress you. Now you're the mother, and the rule is: Moms rule!

Sanctuary

Wrapped in solitude by a rippling pond. Bundled in bed with the kids and all you can hear is the sound of their breathing. Walking beneath the golden leaves of autumn. Sitting at the back of a tiny country church. In a coffeehouse in a city where you don't know a soul. Throwing pots in your studio, covered with clay. Running through sea foam at sunrise. Climbing the steps of the last standing temple and feeling the hush collect in your bones. Resting in water. Dancing alone in a room full of mirrors. Lying on the grass within earshot of a waterfall. Waiting in silence in the hospital chapel. Hidden in the thicket in the hot noonday sun. High on a hill. Low by the marsh. In your kitchen, cooking, cooking. In the garden, picking peas. Lost in the city where no one will find you. Deep in your sanctuary, mother's retreat.

Sand

Sing the praises of sand! Bare feet love to walk in it, footprints love to lie in it, and babies love to collect it in the most unlikely places. Add pails, shapes, sticks, shells, shovels, and water, and you have hours of child-appropriate, mother-approved entertainment at your toe-tips. What age group isn't mesmerized by building castles, intricate tunnels and moats, bridges and walkways and chambers all doomed to tidal destruction? A sandbox is the perfect place for practicing numbers and letters with a stick. A reusable board for playing tic-tac-toe, hangman, and all those games that kids love to play for hours. Oops! Look out! Here's a chunk of sand in little sister's nose. Wet sand can soothe a sting and dry sand can hide under rugs and mats for hundreds of years undetected. Little hands were made for sand, and mothers' feet were made to slip out of shoes and slip into warm, cool, wet, dry sand.

Save

Save the first shoes and the first tooth and the locks from the first haircut. Save those yellowed birth announcements; save the wristband from the hospital. Save the first drawing and the second and the third, and keep saving them until you realize you can't save everything. If fire was approaching, what would you save? Save time out of every day to create the moments that will never be forgotten. Save room in your schedule to do nothing at all. Save that sack of tiny kittens from the dumpster and take them to the shelter where you know they'll be saved. Save the scraps from your last project and recycle them into something you won't throw away. Save that wrapping paper! Save that receipt! Please save some juice for your sister! When it seems that around you, mothers are losing the battle, the one saving grace is you can still save yourself.

Schmutz

It will follow you for the rest of your life. As soon as you put on a beige linen skirt, it will appear. The photographer is poised to snap the once-in-a-lifetime family portrait, and it mysteriously sprouts on the cheek of your toddler. Schmutz is everywhere. It shows up in all flavors: peanut butter, chocolate, strawberry, bubble gum, mud. You'll find it hiding on the backs of elbows and smeared across necks and ground into your brand-new carpet. The moment the hands are clean, they're filthy. As soon as you wipe it up, it's back. Lipstick on your teeth is schmutz. Peanut butter tinged with jelly in your daughter's hair is schmutz. Anything that has escaped from a nose eventually turns into schmutz. Faces are scrubbed and hair is combed and clothing is clean as a whistle. The next thing you know, it's all gone to schmutz!

Seashore

Momma gathered shells by the seashore while the children ran wildly through the waves and the men read the Sunday paper. She always seemed younger near the ocean, with her hair loose and blowing in the wind. Momma all but giggled when she lowered the straps of her bathing suit and Papa slathered lotion all over her back. Maybe it was the endless horizon and the hot sand underfoot that softened her. Maybe it was the absence of routine. We had a kitchenette in our cottage, and we all got our breakfast when we wanted. We had lunch on the sand straight out of the cooler, and more often than not, dinner was at a beachfront restaurant with special deals for kids. Every day, the years slipped from Momma's face and a girlish glow returned to her cheeks. Sometimes when I looked her way, I saw a carefree young woman with a bucket of shells, hardly my momma at all.

Secrets

The secret to life is that there is no secret. The secret to enlightenment is just to start lightening up. The secret to getting in the house without keys is to go through the north cellar window after you pry off the screen. The secret to getting kids to read more is to read along with them. You can ask a child to keep a secret for a day or two, but never, ever ask a child to carry a lifetime of secrets. You can put a lot of time into trying to keep secrets from others, but you'll never keep the tiniest secret from yourself. If it needs fixing or opening, the secret is either duct tape, staples, or a bent paper clip. The secret ingredient in the world's best key lime pie? If everyone knew, it wouldn't be a secret! You know the mom with the three sets of triplets? All I can say is, "It's a secret."

Security

You can spin your wheels every day of your life and security will still elude you. You can possess nine kinds of insurance and four money market accounts and three homes, and wonder why you still feel so vulnerable. Security is an illusion. The thought that when you have everything you need you will feel safe and secure is nothing but your mind's fabrication. Seek a different kind of security beyond false images of material safety. Allow yourself to tap the reservoir of safety that lives inside you. That trusts that all is well and your family is secure. Here you find a security based in divine providence rather than the gross national product. Here you access a deeper faith that you will be guided to all that you need. Here, within, your home is secure because that's simply what you know it to be.

Self

Look at yourself in the mirror and repeat these words: "Taking care of myself is not selfish. Taking care of my needs is not selfish. Taking time just for me is not selfish." Tending to your own self-care and nurturing the well-being of your body, mind, and spirit is a gift to the entire family. Self-sacrifice serves no one, especially you. In those wise, ancient words: "If Mama ain't happy, ain't nobody happy!" Your job first and foremost is to take care of yourself. To nourish yourself inside and out. To maintain a strong sense of who you are even in the midst of the demands of mothering. Somewhere in the schedule, there must be time for you. Right now, go to the mirror and repeat these words: "Taking care of myself is not selfish. Taking care of my needs is not selfish. Taking time just for me is not selfish." Make it your business: Take care of yourself.

Separation

Sometimes the more you are apart, the closer you become. Rather than a notorious source of unbridled anxiety, separation can teach a comforting lesson. Deeply bonded love is not threatened by minutes or months or miles. Heart connections remain firm no matter where bodies are placed on the landscape.

The dance of mother and child needs space so each partner can stretch and push and test her or his own edges.

So each can come to know where mother leaves off and child-self begins. If your child never explores the emptiness between you, how can she learn how to fill it with other things? How can he discover the rich stew of resources that surrounds him? You can adore your child and hold your child close, and still offer the gift of separation. Let yourselves dance in the space you share between you. You might be astonished at how close you can be.

Settle

Settle into a rhythm that honors your need for structure and includes a touch of spontaneity, too. Settle the baby for naptime before you settle into the garden. When you borrow money from your children, settle your debt promptly. That way, you can borrow again. Settle misunderstandings before everybody settles into bed. If the kids can't settle it among themselves, settle things quickly so everybody settles down before dinner. Settle that ridiculous situation at work so your nerves at last will settle down. Don't settle for less when you know you're worth more. Settle into a rainy Sunday with hazelnut coffee and the pile of travel brochures you've been collecting forever. When you get to that picture of the English country cottage with the thatched roof and sheep in the yard, cry, "We're going! It's settled! Once and for all!"

Share

Share a tender secret with your daughter when she's twelve. Promise never to share it with anyone else. Break your chocolate chip cookie into lots of pieces and let everyone have a taste. Show that there's always plenty to share. Share a joke in the bathtub. Blow bubbles under water when you laugh. Share a scary ghost story around a blazing fire. Get together with other moms in the neighborhood and make a list of all the things that you can share. Then everyone doesn't need to have her own. Take turns watching the toddlers. Share your subscription to a favorite magazine—as long as no one takes more than her share of the coupons. Find a way to share some private time with each of your children. Share a walk or a movie or a special afternoon. That way they understand early what it means to have their share.

Shimmering

When the world bangs up against you dull and harsh, bathe yourself in shimmering light. See it violet, indigo, silver satin. Feel its comforting warmth shimmer from the crown of your head to the tip of your toes. Imagine your whole being surrounded by a glow of shimmering stars and bands of celestial glitter. Study the shimmer of a rainbow, glistening with sunlight and dewdrop. Play with shimmery ribbons and glimmery fabrics made into crowns and draped over baby shoulders, and twirl around in circles to a shimmery song. Shower yourself 'neath a shimmery moon. Lie nose-to-nose with a newborn: do you see the shimmering lovelight in her eyes? Hang shimmering curtains at the windows, sun-catchers and prisms that spin a shimmer around the room. See yourself drink from a shimmering river until you're spreading shimmer from the inside out.

Shoulders

You should never be without shoulders. They provide a perfect perch for burping babies and are absolute necessities for holding up shirts. Where else could you possibly drape a kitchen towel or hang a twenty-pound diaper bag? There's no better place for a small child to be when she wants to jam her fingers in your eyes. Or see the Memorial Day parade go by. When you need a shoulder to cry on, find one that's easier to reach than your own. And offer the same for a friend. You can sling a baby backpack over your shoulders and hike eighteen miles into the backcountry. But first, convince yourself that you should. If you believe it's your job to carry the world on your shoulders, you should quit without notice today. If you believe you should shoulder everyone's burdens, you really should rethink those shoulds.

Show

Give your child a lot more show and a lot less tell.
Show him what it looks like to express all kinds of
feelings in a safe and healthy way. Show her the
difference between a regular screwdriver and a
Phillips head. Show your children generosity.
Show them trust in yourself and in others. Show
a three-year-old how to dial 911. Every day, show
through your actions how to respect the Earth
and all who live on it. Let a child see you sweat,
so they know it's OK. Let another adult see you
tremble, so you know it's OK. When you live
your life fully from your heart and not by some
ancient rules, you become a walking example for
everyone around you. And without a single word,
it shows.

Silence

Shhhhh! Can you hear it? The awesome sound of
nothing at all. No crying, no yelling, no whining,
no videos, no vrooom-vrrooom of make-believe
motorcycles. No beeps, bells, buzzers. No questions, no answers, no endless discussion. Shhhhh!
Can you hear it? Sometimes you can fill up an
entire house with the sound of silence. You can
pull it up around you like a cotton blanket right
off a sun-drenched clothesline, and wrap yourself
in silence. Creating silent moments is an art that's
worthy of pursuit. Practice silence. At first, you
may seek to fill the emptiness with something,
anything at all. In time, you will come to savor
the silence and recognize its rich fullness. Find
time for the awesome sound of nothing at all.
Make space for silence. Let it wash over you and
nourish you softly. Shhhhh! Not a word. Can you
hear it?

Simple

Easy. Uncomplicated. No snaps, no zippers, no laces. No small parts. No batteries. No assembly required. Needs no mixing. Ready in minutes. All-in-one. Lifetime warranty. No credit check necessary. No paperwork. No fees, no finance charges, no interest. No sticky fingers. Cannot be swallowed. Wash in hot, cold, or warm water. Never iron. Always in fashion. Wash and wear. One size fits all. No wax, no tarnish. Magically cleans itself. Wipe with a damp cloth. Pull on, pull off. Cheerfully replaced with no questions asked. No shoes, no shirt, no service. The customer is always right. We pay all shipping. Satisfaction guaranteed or double your money back. Safe for nursing mothers. Never tested on animals. Grown without chemicals. No added MSG. We deliver. Please, no tipping. This one's on the house. Whatever you want. When do you want it? Please. Thank you. Amen.

Sisters

Motherhood is an initiation into a vast club that has existed for all time. Suddenly, you feel a kinship with every mother who has ever lived. It's a sisterhood that goes beyond bloodlines or personal history. You take your place in the endless lineage of mothers. You look at the woman with four little ones and the baggy sweat-shirt and the unkempt hair, and see her with greater compassion. You sit with a woman afraid and confused by her reproductive choices, and lose your concretized judgment. Every mother now is your sister. The woman who lives with her baby on the street. The princess who became a single mom. The mother frantically juggling her high-profile job and her love for her daughters. Under the skin, all are your sisters. You are every mother who ever has had a child or lost a child, adopted a child or raised another mother's child. Every mother is your sister. Every mother is you.

Sky

Make time to stare at the sky. Take in its vast-
ness—try to imagine how it feels to live without
limitation. Did you ever notice how the sky blankets us, embraces us from above yet never
smothers us? What's good for the sky is good for
a mother. Spend time with the sky in all kinds of
weather, at all times of day and night. Watch it
move from dark to light, from blue to purple to
red, orange, and gold. Find a horse in a billowing
cloud; see a wagon with wheels flying high. Shriek
and scream at lightning that fills the sky on a
warm summer evening, at thunder that rumbles
right down to your toes. Stargaze and find your
place in an unending universe. The sky helps you
remember how big life can be. How small are the
details. And how starry-eyed we sometimes must
be, to think ourselves the center of it all.

Sleep

Oh! What greater joy than a twelve-hour sleep! A long winter's nap of sweet slumber! Imagine yourself nestled in a bed all your own, with room to toss and turn to your heart's content. No sparring for pillows, no tangling up in arms and legs and stuffed animals and windup toys and bits of crumbling graham crackers. To sleep with curtains drawn and doors locked, unaware that day and night are trading places in the unending sky. To know that no alarm will disturb your sleep, no cries, no whimpers, no crashing, clattering, barking symphony of endless noise. Mom? I'm sleeping. Mom? I'm resting. Mom? I can't hear you. To roll over and drift back into a deep and peaceful sleep. Perchance, to dream without waking until dreaming is done. What you would give for such a heavenly sleep. How you would revel in such a rapturous rest. Shh. Don't wake Mommy. She's sleeping.

Slow

Ever see those street signs that say "Slow/Children
at Play?" They impart a deeper message than just
traffic safety. Children have a way of whipping
things into a frenzy and dragging mothers,
fathers, and small animals along with them.
Youngsters might be little, but they have a
powerful ability to put pedal to the metal and rev
up every aspect of daily (and nightly) living. Since
you're the one with the license to mother, ease up
and slow down. Slow down! Set your cruise
control on nice and easy and leave it there. Do
whatever it takes to slow down the pace. You are
in the driver's seat. You are in control. Simplify,
pare down, streamline. Although you may not
know it from looking around you, there is a pace
somewhere between living a cloistered, monastic
life and whirling your way through existence on a
never-ending merry-go-round. Find that pace and
the peace it brings.

Slurp

Once in a while, take leave of your senses and slurp! Make those silly slurping sounds that drive moms crazy, and watch the kids get wide-eyed in wonder. Slurp soda through a straw. Slurp your tomato soup from a spoon. Slurp up the longest strand of spaghetti you can find in the bowl. Then slurp up the sauce with your tongue. "Mom! That's gross!" Start a slurping contest to see who can slurp the longest, the loudest, the slurpiest. "Mo-o-m!" Let the cat slurp up the spilled milk. Let the horse slurp syrup off your finger. Slurp up your soda and then hold the straw stuck on your tongue. Be a championship slurper. Run your straw around the bottom of your cup like a heavy-duty vacuum and slurp up every last drop of your chocolate mocha milkshake. Let the secret out with a big, long slurp: Mom is the queen of the slurpers!

Soft

Hush! In a toughen-up world, mothering is a gateway to softness. You drop your hard lines and soften your edges the moment a baby is placed in your arms. With every day you spend together, your heart softens. What could be softer than a perfect baby's behind? What caress could be more heavenly than the touch of a tiny hand upon your cheek? What light, balmy breeze compares with the softness of baby's breath? Infants offer a world of soft. Flannel blankets and cotton sleepers and soft toys and the sweet, gentle nuzzle of an afternoon nap. Soft arms around your neck and soft lips upon tender breasts. Even the ordinary takes on a new softness. You can get lost in the eros of laundry! The sound of soft snoring wafts over you like a symphony of whispered murmurings. You may never again know such softness. Tread lightly. Walk slowly. Be soft.

Songs

Sing your own song and invite everyone to sing along. Sing nursery rhymes and folktales from the Old Country and rock-a-bye lullabies that you make up as you go. It doesn't matter how you sound—only that you sing! Go to your favorite house of worship and raise your voice in song. Sing prayers and hymns and sing Elizabethan rounds with anyone who will follow. Remember the theme songs of your favorite shows? Sing them during inexplicable bursts of musical expression. If they don't like your singing, sing louder! Sing the alphabet song until you just can't sing it again. Sing a morning wake-up song and a getting dressed song and a song reciting the schedule of the day. Sing a sad song. Sing the blues. Sing your heart out and sing yourself to sleep. When the kids announce that they're sick of your singing, sing them an operatic get-well tune.

Sorrow

Every mother has her share. It may be a string of small sorrows, small hurts that one after another peck at a mother's heart. It might be one great sorrow that swoops down and takes you in its talons, rising up and enveloping you even as you think you have it tamed. Sorrow goes hand-in-hand with joy, often in equal measure. The mother who feels the rapture of unspeakable joy may also encounter unbearable sorrow. Invite sorrow in with a warm welcome. Give her a place to sit by the fire; she may need to linger a lifetime. Speak with her, cry with her, grieve with her—yet do not push her away. Sorrow is a teacher. At times stern and unrelenting, she will dole out her lessons as you are able to receive them. She will work with you tirelessly. Slowly, as sure as the sun rises, you will make your way to the enduring light at the center of sorrow.

Soup

There comes a time when only soup will suffice.
Your Nana's homemade chicken soup. That
tomato soup you always had with grilled cheese
sandwiches when you were a kid. Thick, hearty
minestrone that you get from the corner deli.
Mulligatawny, zuppa di pesce, avoglomeno,
menudo, borscht. Soup winds around your bones
and finds its way into every nook and cranny of
your soul and warms you from the inside out.
Soup is as comfortable as a bear hug and twice as
soothing. It quiets down cranky children and
anxious adults, and gets the thumbs-up for supper
when nothing else will do. When a sandwich is
too much and a salad too little, soup hits the
sweet spot. Steaming in bowls and mugs, tickling
noses and warming hands, soup offers pure love
in every spoonful and a meal in every can. For
super-duper suppers, there's nothing like soup.

Sparkle

You may be exhausted and you may be wearing your sweats for the fourth straight day, but that doesn't mean you've lost your sparkle. Look at how that little one lights up at the sight of your smile. Feel the way everyone takes on a glow the moment you enter the room. The sparkle never disappears, though it often goes into hiding. Bring out the glitter and the face paint and the polish and the sun-catchers and the prisms and put some strength behind your sparkle. Add sparkles to your denim work shirt and wear sparkly earrings to story time at the library. Watch while everyone else tracks your glistening rainbows across the ceiling and onto the floor. See how everyone sparkles! Dab some sparkles onto your cheeks (as long as no one is licking them). Spend less time staring in the mirror and more time looking into the eyes of the ones you love most. Then stand back! Get ready! Now sparkle!

Spirit

You are more than just a mind and a body. Be
sure to nurture your spirit, too, and the miracles
will follow. Choose a spiritual path that brings
you balance and joy. Remember that you are a
spiritual being living a human life; not a human
being living a spiritual life. Make room and
welcome spirit into your heart. Set a place at your
table for your God, Goddess, Creator, Divine
Master, or Christ. The form is yours to choose.
Find the living spirit in the earth, its flowers,
trees, sky, and rain. Look into the eyes of your
child, your husband, your partners, your
friends—and see radiant spirit looking back at
you. Find your personal relationship with Spirit
and nurture it well. Dance, sing, pray, listen,
make a joyful noise and let Spirit move through
you in loving, magnificent ways. Maintain proper
order: tend first to matters of spirit, and the material takes care of itself.

Spontaneity

Pack up the car, we're going to Vegas! Turn off the oven, we're doing Chinese! Take off your jeans, let's go dressed in formal! Dig out the shovels, let's head to the beach! On the way to work, you took in a movie. Forgot the school conference, went fishing instead. The carpool was boring, you tried karaoke. While the gas tank was filling, you dyed your gray red! So much for the omelet; you had ice cream for breakfast. Topped it with syrup and nuts from your purse. You walked off your job at 10 past 11; by 4:25 you found three that were worse! By 5:45 you were learning to blacksmith. Auditioned for comedy night and brought down the house. Traded your computer for a weekend in Paris. Attended town council dressed up as a mouse. You swung by the bowling alley on the way to the prom. Witness the birth of Spontaneous Mom!

Spring

Just when you think the icy grip of cabin fever will never let you go, here comes spring in all its blossoming, blooming beauty. Time to pull away soggy leaves and find the crocus waking up underneath. Time to watch mother birds carry home strings and twigs and worms for hungry babies. Turn off the TV and tune into spring. Trade winter parkas for jackets and snow boots for sneakers and bring out the kites and the big rubber balls. Soon you'll be setting up the sprinkler! Sweep off the screen porch and wipe off the wicker. Start seeds indoors in window gardens and outdoors, watch for wildflowers. Introduce your little ones to pussy willows and tadpoles and tricycles and afternoon naps in the sun. Buy sunhats and sunglasses and Yes! time for sandals. Whatever is happening, wherever you are; sweep off the deck! It's spring!

Stand

Remember who you are and stand in the place that is yours. Remember what you stand for and how you came to stand for it and make certain that others understand. Stand up to the bully who has the mistaken belief that he holds power over you. Stand in your own place of power and you'll never have to step on others' toes. Stand firm when you know you are right. Stand tall when you know truth is yours. Stand up for your children, especially when they are in danger of standing alone. Stand in protection, in support, in solidarity. Stand beside your teenager in court. Stand up in front of the entire school board if you must. Stand alongside your partner when the show of support matters most. Stand your ground no matter what is huffing and puffing and trying to blow you off course. Sometimes a tree needs to bend in the wind, but the strongest are always left standing.

Start

Start over. Empty everything from your plate and start from the beginning. Dump out the contents of your drawers and start clearing away all that excess. Start the turkey early in the day so you can start eating before it's dark. Focus your energy on a single idea and start a quiet revolution. Don't start a conflagration! Just allow things to get started. Start your children on mother's milk and you give them the best start that there is. Start a support network for working mothers who travel each day to the city. Start slow; start small. Homework gets started as soon as the dishes are done; then get the bathwater started. Let's start a bakery for kids! Let's start a secondhand store for moms and babies. Don't wait another minute to start. Can't you feel that it's time to get started?

States

Like a cross-country trucker, you travel through states all the time. State of confusion. State of exhaustion. State of grace. Although the signs are obvious, sometimes you miss them and it's hard to know exactly what state you're in. State of bliss? State of madness? State of Minnesota? Eternal state of unknowing? More often than not, the state you're in is nothing more than a pass-through to your next destination. It's where you are now, yet you can take heart in knowing that your time in that particular state is nearly over. You may be taking a detour through a state of anxiety, and your state of calm is just around the corner. Don't be in too much of a hurry to leave the state you're in. In the blink of an eye, a fluid or gaseous state can change into a solid state of well-being.

Stay

Here are the rules about staying: You stay at home with your baby as long as it works for everyone involved. You stay in the hospital as long as your insurance company says it's OK. The baby stays on breastmilk until it feels right to do something different. Your toddler stays at home until you want to put him in day care, and he stays as long or as little as you like. School-aged children can stay overnight during the school week, as long as everyone agrees it's OK. They can stay out playing baseball till dark in the summer, unless all the parents say otherwise. Moms can stay out as late as they want—assuming they've hired a sitter. It's OK to stay for a second feature, but if you don't call ahead, you're grounded for good. The gerbils are welcome to stay here forever—but the cage that they live in had better stay clean.

Stop

Stop it right now. Stop thinking that you're a terrible mother. Stop comparing yourself to that woman on the radio or that woman down the hall or that woman who seems so utterly perfect at everything. Stop checking in with nine so-called experts and a pile of books for every little thing, and start listening to your own intuition. Stop thinking that you're the only one who sometimes feels confused or alone or utterly overwhelmed, and start finding other mothers who understand what you're going through. Stop for just a moment and behold the marvelous gift that is your child. The marvelous creation that is your life as a mother. Stop and breathe in and then breathe out. And again. And again. If you can't stop to feel yourself breathing, you're going way too fast.

Stories

Mama always loved her stories. They rose up out of her just before bedtime, needing scarcely a hint of invitation. Stories sent us to sleep and warmed our insides when the lights went out and we could only sit in the dark and listen. She wove tales of dinosaurs searching for water and fairies who rode golden horses in the forest, and always, the stories her mama told her. It seemed like her stories never ended. When you thought she was finished, she would pull the rug out from under you and leave you hanging until the next chapter. Happy endings never mattered to Mama. In her stories, farms failed and villages burned and powerful kings lost their power. Gypsies danced barefoot and fishermen's boats ran into squalls and forever remained in the watery deep. I've seen lots of movies since I was a kid, but nothing ever matched Mama's stories.

Strength

You're stronger than you know. If it meant that your child would live, you could pick up a small truck and toss it over your shoulder. You've withstood attacks from all directions and all manner of enemies seen and unseen—and you're still standing. Maybe you're not the strongest disciplinarian in town, but you've got what it takes to keep that wild bunch in line. You've endured more than some triathletes will ever know, and you did it without a personal trainer. When the world stopped turning, you were the pillar of strength for the family. You've been working your heart muscle for years, and now you can flex it in any situation. Add up all the bags of groceries and sacks of kitty litter and loads of dirty laundry you've lugged around over the years, and give yourself a gold medal. You prove every day that you're strong.

Stretch

Shift your life in powerful ways with just a bit of stretching. Expand your mind with a little more intellectual stimulation and wrap your brain around new ideas. Try a book club, a discussion group, a lecture series, a workshop. Stretch your body gently and then find yourself moving into yoga, dancing, swimming. It's not too much of a stretch to widen your circle of acquaintances, is it? Take a step toward making one new friend. You won't strain something by reaching further into alternative ways of healing, will you? Stretch your thinking about energy work, about the healing power of color, light, and sound. Expect some stretching from your children, too. They can take on more responsibility and make greater contributions to the family, whatever their ages. You can limber up without donning leotards.

Take a deep breath and now s-t-r-e-t-c-h.

Struggle

Does it feel you've been struggling forever? If you haven't been struggling to make ends meet, you've been struggling to balance your family, yourself, and your job. You've been struggling to discover your true nature and the work you were put here to do. You've been struggling to live joy in a world filled with fear. Right now, feel that the struggle is over. Close your eyes and find an internal peace where struggle no longer exists. Feel your shoulders drop as you release years of struggle. It's over. See your spine straightening and your neck lengthening as your burden lightens. It's gone now. *Struggle*: erase the word from your mind and banish the feeling from your body. You choose. Write a goodbye letter to the struggles you're leaving behind. Tell them thanks for the memories, but it's time to hit the road. And tell struggle not to come back. No more, no more, no more.

Success

Achieving success isn't nearly as hard as defining it. Is it the house of your dreams in the neighborhood of your dreams, filled with the furniture of your dreams? Is it money in the bank and a solid investment portfolio and a prestigious position at a high-profile firm? Are you successful when your child aces the SAT and brings home the MVP award? Left alone to ponder, how would you define *success*? Might it be as humble as rebuilding your credit after divorce handed you a bankruptcy? Could your version of success include working for yourself, at your own pace, creating something useful with your own heart, hands, and head? Or maybe success for you is even simpler: A peaceful day. A nourishing sit-down meal at a freshly wiped table. An afternoon nap beside someone you love. The key to success is in knowing this adage: The only standards to go by are your own.

Supporters

If you ever feel like you're walking a lonely journey, imagine a meeting of all your supporters. Call up images of everyone who supports you. See the room fill up with their smiles. The family members who help keep you afloat when times are tight. The friends who help you hold your dreams and push you back on track when you slip. Support by any other name is still support. Some supporters gently comfort you when you need a little TLC. Others kick your butt and give you a boost out of a personal darkness that doesn't want to quit. Remember that woman who shopped at your store every day just because she liked you? Or that man who wrote you the kindest letters after reading about you and your kids in the local news? In your imagination, look each one in the eye. Give gratitude for all they have done. And feel uplifted by their support.

Surprise

Surprise everyone with hot fudge sundaes for dinner, and then let them surprise you by doing the dishes. Surprise yourself by calling in sick to work and taking a Mom's Day Off, then astonish yourself by spending half the day alone at the movies and the other half sipping green tea and eating scones with a woman who is doing the same. Surprise! Wear violet when everyone else is in black. Surprise! Pick the kids up two hours early and stop by the park for hula hoops and hotdogs. Surprise! Take your favorite adult away for the weekend and surprise your teenager by putting him in charge. Next time they ask, surprise them all by saying yes. Next time, surprise! the answer is no. Ditch your old flannel nightgown for something silky and sexy, and when your beloved asks, "What's going on?" smile sweetly and just say, "Surprise."

Surrender

The mothering journey is so large that you can never quite wrap your brain around it. So don't even try. Surrender to the twists and turns that present themselves. Know that no amount of thinking will guide you through this territory. You have been told so much about mothers, and this is what you must surrender. The notion that good mothers are with their children twenty-four/seven. The myth of mother as sacrificial martyr, giving every last drop of herself for her progeny. Surrender these images so that others may emerge. The mother that is you may be unrecognizable. The mother that aches to be freed from within your bones may only come forth through surrender. When you stop trying to work it so hard, then you surrender. When you get out of your own way, you will meet your mothering self face-to-face. The only map to carry is surrender.

Surround

Surround yourself with a cocoon of well-being and watch your life transform before your very eyes. Create a home that offers pockets of peace, quiet islands in a turbulent sea. Surround yourself with natural fibers, whispering tones, green plants, and soothing wind chimes that move with the slightest breeze. Cover the television screen when it's not in use, and keep the volume low when it is. Clear your surroundings of clutter so that tabletops and floors and counters and people can breathe. Mist the air with essential oils and light the room with aromatherapy candles. Establish quiet times for reading, resting, and relaxation and make a commitment to honor those times. Fill your surroundings with the things, people, and energy that support you and your family's well-being. Energized and active. Subdued and calm. Free and easy. Create your most balanced surroundings without, and create greater balance within.

Sweat

Work it, Momma! Run and jump, cycle or skip, dance and swing. Do whatever it takes to sweat! Not perspire, not lightly glow, but good old-fashioned, let-the-BO-flow, sweat! Show your children how to get up out of the chair and get up out of the car and run up a few flights of stairs with a baby on your back. Or one stair if that's where you start. Get out and pant and show them what Mom is really made of! Rototill the garden and come back drenched in sweat. Hike a mountain trail at high noon in August and show them the meaning of sweat. Hang on a ladder for hours until you're spattered with a mixture of paint and sweat. Clean out your pores and flush out your toxins and feel the sweet scent of your sweat.

Swing

You don't have to be seven to savor a swing. There's something about having your feet off the ground and your face in the sun that can melt away stress in a minute. Swing high or swing low. Swing fast or swing slow. Sit on a swing and be as still as you can, and enjoy hardly swinging at all. Take your little one on a swing and feel the tightness of the day slip out of both of you. Curl up alone on a wooden porch swing and feel in your belly why babies love swings. Rock yourself gently to your own rhythm. Swing yourself to the clouds, to the moon, and to a soft quiet slumber. Swing as high in the sky as you dare, then swing yourself back to your center. Can you smooth out your mood swings on the seat of a swing? Like a pendulum that's tired of swinging to extremes, slow down, slow quiet, slow swing.

Take

How much can you take? Take a moment to take a deep breath. Take a five-minute break. Take it slow before you take it too much further. When you feel you just can't take it any longer, take a shower. Don't take more than your share, but if you deserve it, you can take it all. Take the kids to the county fair and take a ride on the old carousel. Take it nice and easy. Shine up that old baby carriage you got for a song at a yard sale, and take it out for a spin. Take a number. Take your turn. Take off. Take a couple of pounds off before summer. When nobody's looking, you can take the last piece of candy. Take the whole gang out to the ball game, and take your glove in case a wild foul comes your way. Take the fly, take a bow, and take your place in history as a major league mom.

Takeout

Isn't this what civilization is about? After a nightmare of a day, you drive up to a box and talk with a squawking voice you barely understand. You fish around in your purse for some money and before you get out of the parking lot, you've got dinner! You've got meat, you've got potatoes, you've got sushi and noodles. You've got drinks and desserts. You've got dinner! Take it out of the car, take it through the garage, and take credit for bringing home the bacon, lettuce, and tomato. The pizza, the bread sticks, the moo goo gai pan. Take it all out of the bag, take it over to the table, and take the wet wipes and napkins when you're finished. Take your belt out another notch, take out the trash, and take a moment to give thanks for takeout. You can always take time out for takeout.

Talk

You need to have that talk immediately. You need to sit your daughter down and talk about those grades. You need to talk to your son about his new friends. It's time to have a heart-to-heart talk with your neighbor about the dogs. Talk about a mess! It's gone way past time to have an honest conversation about the mix-up with your property taxes. That talk about the birds and bees with your sixth-grader? Way past time and you know it. How about your own talk with your gynecologist? Haven't you been meaning to talk about that lump? Talk about being a procrastinator! Wasn't that a wonderful talk you had last Sunday with the Monsignor? You could have talked and talked for hours. So what if people are talking about your new pickup truck? Let them talk all they want. It's nothing but talk.

Taste

You're getting closer and you can taste it. There's energy all around and you taste it. Someone offered you rattlesnake cakes last night, and you found yourself willing to taste it! Your tears are salty; your milk is sweet. Sweat drips down your face and you taste it. The kids made you pudding with flour and beans—and Oy! How could you not taste it? Three hours later, you're brushing your teeth and the fact is, still, you can taste it. Quick, grab the baby. She's headed for the dog dish. She sees kibbles and she wants to taste it. Your lips were awakened with minty-fresh kisses and it makes you smile again just to taste it. They sprayed all the lawns with some chemical goo, and you swear that still you can taste it. You've planted your seeds and the harvest is coming. It's not mental, you know. You just taste it.

Tea

What comfort is found in a single cup of tea.
Sipped with another or sipped alone, tea offers an
oasis of calm midst the raging storms of a hectic
day. Tea with scones, tea with cookies, tea with
conversation. Something about tea opens you up
and leads you into gentle contemplation. Every sip
is a step toward serenity. Mothers' secrets are
shared over tea; mothers' stories are spun over tea.
Honest and unadulterated tea can lead you back
to center and bring balance wherever you're
needing it most. Whether served in china cups
with silver spoons or partaken in paper on a park
bench. Whether fresh-brewed, whole-leaf tea
with exotic origins, or a bag that you picked up in
a motel in Davenport. Steaming tea made with
leaves and roots and berries can be your afternoon
confidante or your nighttime companion. When
you need a reason to stop, breathe, and listen, be
sure to take time for tea.

Teach

You don't need a Ph.D. to know that children are the greatest teachers on the planet. So while you're instructing the finer points of ABC and 1-2-3, remember that you're the student, too. Like a powerful young Buddha, your child will teach you immeasurable depths of patience, unconditional love, and forgiveness—if only you are willing to learn. As you teach your little one the art of tying her shoes nice and tight, she's teaching you the art of loosening up and letting go. Teaching how to put things in order? He's teaching you to appreciate the wild beauty of chaos. You are your child's first teacher, so focus on the life lessons that count: Live from the heart. Follow your bliss. Play well with one another. Never judge a book by its cover. Let the force be with you. And most important of all: Life is the school; love is the lesson.

Tell

When it's time, tell your child the story of his birth. Tell her what it meant to have your love transformed into a living, breathing baby girl. Tell him how much it hurt to give birth, and tell him you wouldn't have traded it for anything in the world. Tell stories until someone falls asleep, even if that someone is usually you. Tell your daughter it wasn't her fault; tell your son it's not his burden to bear. Tell everyone you love them at least ten times as often as you tell them to pick up their toys. Look at yourself in the mirror and tell yourself what a beautiful mother you are. Ask your beloved to tell you the same. Wonder how a five-year-old can tell the same joke over and over and over, and fall down laughing every time. Promise to tell the truth, the whole truth, and nothing but the truth. When no one is talking, tell the kids that they don't have to tattle. But tell them they do have to tell.

Thank-Yous

It means so much to hear they're grateful. That they appreciate all you do. The thank-yous come on notebook paper, scribbled in pink and red and blue. A cup of tea can be a thank-you. A jar of flowers says thank you, too. **Thanks for being my special Mom,** and thanks for all the things you do. Thanks come in every size and shape. They always touch a tender spot. Thanks for picking me up on Sunday. Thanks for your trust, Mom. Thanks a lot! You can never hear too many thank-yous. E-mail, snail mail, voice mail, too. Cookies and drawings and painted seashells. All designed to say, **"Thanks, Mom. I love you."**

Think

Think that you've got the most beautiful children in the entire world. Think you're married to the most wonderful creature who ever walked the earth. Think that you're looking mighty fine for your age. Think that you're doing OK. Think that you'll make it this time. Think how much better off you are than most. (If you don't think that's true, think again.) Think long and hard about changing your job or your address or your custom window treatments. Think twice before agreeing to the overnight beach trip after the prom. (Think that you might be crazy even to think about it.) Lie in bed all night thinking about starting a business. Think about marketing, about traffic flow, about inventory, about profits. Think that sleeping would be a fine thing to do. Then think yourself into slumber.

Tie

Help her tie her shoes in double knots so she won't trip. Help him tie his tie on prom night and hope that he learns to tie better than you. Tie up her ponytails and pigtails with brightly colored ribbons and bows, and tie a bit of color in your hair, too. Tie up the phone for hours, telling Grandma and Grandpa about the lost tooth, the triple play, and the new family who moved in upstairs. Tie a helium balloon to a wrist or a stroller or a backpack so it doesn't blow away. Tie bells on doors so you can hear little ones coming and going. Telecommute and avoid the daily traffic tie-ups on the freeway. Keep family ties intact, yet loose enough so everyone can breathe. Keep your apron strings tied until you're ready to cut them, but not tied so tight that anyone chokes.

Time

Time to wake everyone up. Time to braid hair and tie shoes and button buttons. Time for breakfast, for lunches, for permission slips and checks for baseball and notes to teachers and coaches and baby-sitters. *Where is time for you?* Time to pop in a load of laundry. Time to take dinner out of the freezer. Time to stop by the dry cleaner and the bank and the post office. Just enough time to get to the station. *Where is time for you?* Time for staff meeting. Time for class. Time to pick up the prescriptions. Time to take Goldie to the vet. Time to wait twenty-five minutes on the phone for tech support. *Where is time for you?* Time to make cookies for the Halloween party. Time to send off birthday gifts to the cousins. Time to find a white shirt for the band concert. *Where is time for you?* Just enough time to get to cello lessons, to soccer, to gymnastics, to scouts. To heat up dinner, to help with homework, to watch one favorite show, to fold the laundry, to clean the dishes, to take baths and unbraid hair, to read stories and listen to fears about monsters in the night. *Where is time for you?*

Tissues

Don't leave home without them. You can bag
some in a zip-lock or stuff a wad into your bag,
but always be sure to have tissues. When you've
got runny noses to wipe and muddy toes to clean
and a face covered with chocolate pudding, you'll
be glad you brought the tissues. Tissues mop up
tears at weddings and funerals and reruns of the
sweetest, sappiest movies you've ever seen. Spilled
the juice? Here's a tissue. Bloody nose? Here's
some tissue. Endless drool? Got a tissue (no, wait,
here's a towel). Moms can always find tissues in a
pocket or purse—just in time to wipe makeup off
the face of a misdirected twelve-year-old. The
honey bear tipped over and the ants are having a
picnic of their own? Try this tissue. Your latte is
spilling on the seat of the car? Yikes, a tissue, fast!
And when diapers are dripping on some dusty
dirt road, give thanks you remembered the
tissues!

Today

Right now, be here with today. Today is the small
hand in yours, warmly mittened. Today is the sun
overhead and the clouds rolling in from the east.
Today is the last day and today is the first. Today
is the day you choose something different. Today
is icicles melting in the courtyard. Today is vanilla
hazelnut snow cones and a purple plastic spoon.
Today, the story about the woman who wouldn't
sit in the back of the bus. Today, the green striped
sweater. Today, the conversation about contracep-
tion. Today is the day you sign the papers. Today
is the day Daddy slips in the hall. Today you find
the earring with the pearl you've been missing.
Today is lipstick and heels. Today is naps all day
long. Today the silence is shattered. Today you
become. Today is your knowing. The present is
today.

Tomorrow

Tomorrow picks up where today leaves off.
Tomorrow, the sitter comes. Tomorrow, you'll get
to work early. Tomorrow you'll start those
stretching exercises the doctor gave you.
Tomorrow, you hope, you'll start bleeding. May
the baby sleep through 'til tomorrow. May the war
be over tomorrow. May tomorrow be the day that
the bathroom is finally done. Tomorrow, maybe,
swimming. You'll hang sheets on the clothesline
tomorrow. Hear from your lawyer tomorrow. Oh,
yes, let the check come tomorrow. Tomorrow the
dentist. Tomorrow the taxes. Tomorrow after
school, end-of-year conference. Tomorrow for
dinner, fried chicken. Try out that new deli
tomorrow. Please let it rain tomorrow. If not,
you'll water tomorrow. Clean clothes all around
for tomorrow. School lunch will do for tomorrow.
When today is done, there's always tomorrow.

Touch

Some mothers are born with the touch. They lightly circle a finger around a crying infant's cheek and all becomes quiet. They raise their eyebrows in a most subtle manner and every child within blocks begins to behave. With a little bit of that and a pinch of this, they turn mediocre meals into gourmet delights. In the garden, their touch is green. In front of a classroom, they have the Midas touch of gold. Don't underestimate your touch. Everything that you do touches the lives of those around you. Simply by being who you are, by living your authentic life, you deeply touch others and leave them changed forever. You float down the street, beaming your goodness, and people feel they've been touched by an angel. It's not so much in the fingers, this magical touch. It's a gesture you make from the heart.

Trade

The smartest mothers make the best trades. Trade to save money, to save time, but most of all, trade for fun. Swap child care for chowder. Swap your stroller, your rocker, your baby backpack for website design. Trade those beautiful maternity clothes for theater tickets. Give a day of gardening and get a day of wallpapering. Trade the stationary bike for one that will take you out the door. Trade books you'll never read again for a fresh pile of those you will. Got puppies? Swap them for, um, kittens??? Offer an hour of your skills for a quick hair trim. Trade that ridiculously inappropriate gift certificate for one you can really use. Trade on the Internet or on the bulletin board at the coffee shop or out in the school parking lot. The rules are simple: Be clear about what you want. Be clear about what you don't want. Make a good trade and you've made the day good.

Traditions

Take stock of your family traditions. The gatherings. The outings. The holidays. The meals. Do they continue to strengthen and nourish the golden thread of connection? Or have they slipped into hollow replays of old, tired patterns? The very best traditions grow and change to reflect new lifestyles, even as they honor the ways of the past. Do your children look forward to the annual trip to the family homestead? Or do they dread the stilted conversation and unspoken truths? Are you excited to plan for the traditional holiday season—or are you burdened by old resentments that continue to play out through never-ending drama? Explore lighter, healthier ways to carry on longstanding traditions. Suggest new activities, new foods, new conversations, and greater openness and authenticity. Have the courage to consider radical change as well as minor refinements. If family traditions aren't strong enough to withstand evolution, maybe it's time to create new traditions of your own.

Transcend

When you feel dragged down by circumstance, rise above it. Transcend the drama of the moment and act from a higher place of knowing. Watch others rush around trying to beat chaos into order—and take the high road. If they threaten you with ultimatums, respond from a heightened perspective. When they fling judgment in your face and question your integrity, learn the peace and power of turning the other cheek. There may be glue in the basement, but you don't need to step right in. Lift yourself above the babble of gossip and fear, and find safe refuge until the deluge is over. Observe the anger and pain swirling around you. While others rant and rave, choose to ride out the storm in your own quiet way. Some will choose to see a nightmare; you await an unfolding miracle. Allow yourself to transcend ego and control, especially when it's yours. Why crash around the barnyard with a bunch of crazed chickens? Transcend the clatter and soar with eagles above.

Travel

You may be the rock that holds your family together, but that doesn't mean you can't take an occasional road trip! Go alone or go with your sweetheart. Go with another mom who gets that unscratchable itch every now and then for the open road and an endless supply of gas station snacks. Crank up the CDs and sing along as loud as you want and do all the things you never let the kids do when they're in the car! Go someplace you've never been before and try something different. Even for a day. Cruise into a gallery or a museum or tour an old ship or watch street performers or travel 150 miles to get a massage and a facial. It's not about the destination; it's about the journey! It's about remembering that there are lots of bathrooms you don't have to clean, lots of beds you won't have to make, and lots of great food you can eat with your hands. Now get out of your orbit and travel.

Treasure

This lullaby, this sunset, this child sleeping in your arms. That one yawn, this smile, these fingers intertwined. Treasure what will never come again. This ride on the merry-go-round, these sweet words, this lopsided snow-bunny followed by this cup of cocoa in front of this fire. These are the moments always to treasure. That laugh you shared when the sprinkler went wild. The look he gave you across the gym floor. That one day on the trail, before the bear sent you fleeing down the hill. That afternoon the puppies were born. Those walnut pancakes they served you in bed. Always remember the way she looked that night. Never forget the feeling, how you knew you would lay down your life for the life of this child. Treasure this touch, that glance, these kisses, those hugs. These treasures will last you a lifetime.

Treat

Treat yourself at least as well as you treat your children. Treat yourself to a massage, to a hot fudge sundae, to a barefoot walk in grass or sand or pebbly water. Treat yourself to fifteen minutes of absolutely nothing. **Treat yourself with respect, with honor,** and watch how others do the same. When Halloween rolls around, treat the whole family to something that's more about the season and less about the sweets. Treat another mother to tea and muffins, and know that in time, the treat will come back around to you. Treat every child you meet as though he were your own, for in a way, he is. **Treat yourself to a day on the town,** to the art gallery and the theater and to the sights of the city. Then when you're full, retreat.

Trees

There's a lot to learn from a tree. How to put
down roots in hospitable territory. How to bend
with the wind and weather the storms. How to
send out branches and hold them close until
they're strong enough to send out buds of their
own. A tree flows through the seasons of its life,
never once worrying whether winter will be
followed by spring. Leaves fall when the time is
right, never stressing if it's too late or too early.
Left to its own nature, a tree receives all that it
needs and gives much in return. Trees provide
safe haven. Nourishment for beings smaller than
they are. Solid ground for nesting. When they're
healthy, they stick together without bumping up
against each other so much that one of them gets
hurt. Next time you're near one, it's something to
think about: how much you can learn from a tree.

Trust

Trust yourself. Listen to your intuition, your sixth sense, your voice within, the angels that whisper to you during the night. Whatever you call it, know that you are the source of your greatest wisdom. Trust that your body will know when to birth this baby. Trust that your breasts know how to give your child his first nourishment. Trust that you are cared for by people who hold your best interests at heart. Trust that there is something larger out there, and trust yourself to know what that is for you. Trust that you have maternal instincts, no matter who tells you otherwise. Now trust yourself to rely on those instincts. Trust that your daughter will not enter first grade in diapers. (If she must, trust that she will be surrounded by those who will accept her for who she is.) Trust that you are only given that which you can handle. Now trust yourself to handle it in the very best way you can.

Truth

Sometimes the biggest lie you'll ever hear is the one you tell yourself. You convince yourself everything is perfect, but that's not the truth. You tell yourself you've got everything you always wanted, but that's not the truth either. It's easy to tell the truth, and a lot more challenging to live it. Living your truth means every step you take rings out with the truth of who you are. Your truth flows through your veins and permeates your every thought, word, and deed. You stand in your own truth even when pressed to tell little white lies. Even when you could slide and nobody really would notice. To live your truth, first you must discover it. It might take years, but once you uncover your truth, you never again will live a life of lies. The ribbon of truth is always within your reach. Why don't you reach out and grab it?

Try

When did you give up trying? When was the last time that you stepped out of your comfortable status quo and gave something different a little try? Did you try on a ridiculous pair of shoes just for the fun of it, just to see how they fit? When your discipline tactics were getting you nowhere, did you let it all go and try something radically new? Sometimes things get so trying that you don't want to try anymore. Sometimes it takes less energy to try than never to try at all. What's the harm in trying? Try a little tenderness. Try getting tough. Try putting a little meat back in your diet—or try taking some out. Try that new hair cuttery next to the drive-in. Try going totally blonde. Or try out a weave. You can think, you can wonder, you can try to imagine. But try as you might, you will never know what will happen until you take a try.

Understand

Understand that things are not always what they appear to be—and that you may not always understand. When you feel your children turn away from everything you have offered, understand that is what they must do. Try to understand without judging their actions too harshly. Without taking things personally. Understand that it's not always about you. Understand this: the dance of mothering is one of coming together, moving apart, and returning only to separate again. Do your best to understand that what is right for another mother may not be right for you. Understand and honor what is deliciously different about every mother, and what is the same. Learn to understand with your heart. With compassion and acceptance. With a generosity of spirit and always, with unconditional love. It's not so hard to understand. The challenge is understanding that perhaps you never will.

Unfold

It's beautiful to watch things gently unfold. They open in their own time, with no care as to what fits your schedule. No one ever rushed a rose's unfolding. No one ever commanded a child to talk before she was ready, or to walk before he crawled. A full-term baby was never born in seven months, no way, no how. Everything you do needs time to gestate before unfolding. You can do everything in your power to instill a sense of responsibility in a child, but it won't really take until it's time. Then one day, the seed you planted will gently bear its fruit. When your passion for anything takes hold, it's easy to want to push, to rush, to make things happen in your personal way. Yet even an idea has a life of its own. Like a living being, it has its own unique coding. You can't push the river, so why even try? Sit back and let it unfold.

Vacations

Real ones! Vacations from making all the beds and cooking all the meals and picking up after everyone else. Something that's worth sending home a postcard. A vacation to a part of the state you've never seen, or to a tiny village in Ireland. A mountain retreat. That long-awaited trip to Disneyland. A city vacation that's steeped in culture and music and art every day. A work vacation where everyone helps to renovate the barn and there's not even a movie for miles. A vacation filled with long days of relaxation and you never have to wear hose. An old-fashioned summer of beach and bumper cars and saltwater taffy between your teeth. Give yourself a ski vacation where the powder is fresh and every night you fall into bed aching with joy. Take a vacation from anything that beeps at you, flashes, or calls out your name. Life is short! Don't forget your vacations.

Variety

Routine is a great thing for babies, but it can be oh-so-boring. Spice up the same-old same-old and watch your spirits soar. Slip some salsa into the spaghetti when no one is looking. Slather marmalade onto waffles and serve it for dinner. If everybody knows that Monday's for laundry, shake up their world and wash Wednesday instead. Break out and take an earlier bus. Just once, try Indian instead of Italian. Start dusting to Dvorak and biking to the Beatles. Trade in your car for a horse of a different color. Why? Because it's different. Why? For variety. Why? Because you're boring yourself half to death. This week, have Mom's Night Out on Tuesday and before anyone gets too attached, switch to Saturday noon. Give up the weekend in the country for a ride on the river. If you've always done Manhattan, then try out St. George. Always a camper? Then try out some bowling. Getting stuck in routine is a horrible snore.

Vent

Give yourself ten or twenty minutes and let 'er rip! Vent in the shower where the water will drown out your pity party, or in the car where no one else can hear you, or to a strong individual who can hold the space for you without taking anything personally. Clear the area of impressionable children and adults who just don't get it. When it's safe to begin, let out every bit of anger and resentment that's rolling around inside you. Don't hold back. Liberally sprinkle your diatribe with inappropriate language—the very kind you would never allow from your kids. Tell it exactly like it is and precisely how you expect it to be from here on out. Rage and holler and complain and be as negative and judgmental as you want. Time's up! Take a deep breath, pull yourself together, and walk on refreshed and revived.

Videos

All you moms come out of the closet and come clean! Admit that on one or even two occasions you turned your VCR into a baby-sitter. You've got the entire Disney collection stashed on the shelves of your entertainment center, and that's only the tip of the iceberg! Remember that snowy day last February when you had a huge deadline to meet and the kids were all home with the flu? Remember when Dad returned from duty after three months, and you spent an entire Saturday behind closed doors? Videos are educational, you say. They develop important cognitive skills, you claim. 'Fess up! They save your life when you're too pooped to play and too preoccupied to be present. You've been through six copies of *The Lion King* and the seventh is about to self-destruct. Just goes to show that you never can tell. A houseful of videophiles in our midst!

Vision

Even when it seems that a pile of laundry is blocking your view, hold on to your vision. See it unfolding in a way you can't quite define. Bigger, bolder, brighter than your own imagination. Smaller, warmer, cozier. How does your vision grow? Into a tidy home with a well-tended herb garden? Into a life of service to humanity? Into a greater love than you've ever known? While a goal emerges from the mind, your vision takes root in your heart. It calls to you with a commanding voice, bits and pieces presenting themselves in arrangements that at first may seem unlikely. How does it feel to step into your vision? What do you smell? Taste? Hear? Stay with your vision even if it seems to grow dim. You can never turn your back on that which only you were meant to see.

Visitors

Sometimes you want them, sometimes you don't.
The right visitors can brighten a torturous
morning, fill your fridge with fabulous food, and
play with Junior while you catch up on paperwork
or sleep or both. The wrong ones will moon
around like bored teenagers, insisting you entertain them and throwing a big fat monkey wrench
into your carefully crafted routine. Some visitors
bring bags full of games and socks and a stack of
great books from the library. Others bring the
beginning of strep throat, a cell phone that plays
"Happy Days Are Here Again" every seven
minutes, and a big sack of cheese and crackers for
your dairy-free, wheat-free toddler. You decide,
OK? Who you want. When you want them. And
exactly how long is too long to stay. Be firm, be
polite, and before you answer the door, be
certain. Visitors? Sometimes you want them,
sometimes you don't.

Voice

When you find your authentic voice, use it. Voice your opinions with conviction and quietly listen as others speak theirs. Voice your approval before the vote is taken. Voice your disappointment if it ends in defeat. Speak your needs and wishes clearly, in a voice that everyone around you can understand. Voice your discontent—and voice it again if no one pays attention the first time around. Believe it when you're complimented on your lovely singing voice. Try to get through to your children with the voice of reason. When that doesn't work, the voice of authority will. If you want to get things done, use active voice, not passive. If anyone of any age raises her voice to you in a disrespectful manner, immediately voice your disapproval in a voice she's certain to hear. If you keep your voice silent year after year, don't be one bit surprised that you've lost it.

Vulnerability

I was old myself before I saw my mother display even a hint of vulnerability. She was tough as nails and there wasn't a chink in her armor. She ruled us with an iron hand and a stiff upper lip, and there was never any room for tears. She had no time for foolishness, no welcome for strangers, and not a passing glance would she give to any frailty. When she lost the baby, I thought I saw her staring out the window at the willow tree, but when she saw me in the doorway, she jumped up out of her chair and bustled about with her cleaning. When the movie would start to get mushy, mother found reasons to leave the room until the action resumed. Even when they lost the farm at auction, she stood stoic and managed the adding machine. It was many years to the day that I saw mother soften. She said, "I'm kind of frightened. Could you hand me my cane?"

Wait

Wait another moment. Wait another day. Wait five minutes before you do something you might later regret. What's the harm if you wait? Wait until it's time. You'll know it. Wait until you're ready. You'll feel it. Let the others wait for you for once. Don't spend half your life waiting for something to happen. If you snooze, you're likely to lose. Read a book of well-being for mothers while you wait. Play a silly game while you wait. The kids can cool their jets while you're in the bathroom. They can just wait till you're finished to borrow your phone. The laundry can wait. The dishes can wait. The dusting can most definitely wait. Wait until they're older!

Wait until the terrible twos!

Wait till they start driving!

Just wait till they're in college!

Oh goody! Oh joy! I can't wait.

Walk

The longest journey begins with a single step, so start walking. Forget the elevator and walk! Park in the last row of the parking lot and get in a quick walk on your way to the mall. Walk alone on a dirt road and let your arms swing naturally. Watch how the clouds move in rhythm to your walk. Walk down a crowded sidewalk and make eye contact with everyone who walks by. Walk through your neighborhood and offer blessings and good wishes to every house and business you pass. Take the kids for a walk in all kinds of weather. Let them taste snowflakes on their tongues and hear leaves crackling underfoot and quack like ducks in the rain. With every step, walk like the queen you are. If your legs won't take you walking, walk down an imaginary walkway that lives only in your mind.

Watch

Watch what you're doing. Little eyes are watching you more than you know, so be mindful of all that you model. No matter what you say or how often you say it, what matters is where your feet go walking. Walking your talk means aligning your words with your actions. Saying what you mean and meaning what you say. Showing up the same whether you're kicking back with the kids or kicking butt at the town meeting. Keep an eye on how you speak about others, lest little voices echo everything they hear. For all the times you tell them to watch their language, make sure that you're watching yours. Are you watching along while they watch too much TV? Watching over their shoulders after you told them you trust them? Nobody says that a mom has to be a paragon of virtue. Nobody says you can't slip. Just watch your step. Little feet are following closely behind you.

Water

Ah, sweet elixir for the parched soul! Let it wash over you in waves and running rivulets, in gentle drops and pounding showers of healing rain. Drink it fresh from the spring, with a spritz of lemon, and quench your long, long thirst. Walk barefoot in tingling-cold water to wake up your skin and jolt you out of the everyday. Take baths with your children until they're too old not to; swim with your children like dolphins before they're too cool to consider it. Soak in natural hot springs, in backyard hot tubs, in a relaxing brew of sea salt and sesame oil. Come out of the desert of your days and drink in the moisture that crawls down the greenhouse windows and drips from the white tile of the steam room wall. Admit how much you miss being misted—and commit to miss water no more.

Watermelon

Watermelon is worth its weight in gold. And worth the wait until summer. Put the kids in bathing suits, save the napkins for another day, and bring on the juicy, slurpy, messy melon. Watermelon quenches the thirst of a hot summer day and turns any picnic into a party. Serve it in slices or balls or spooned straight from its own handy bowl. Cool off hot bodies and hot tempers with cool melon. Top off tetherball and tennis and swimming with melon. Watermelon brings in kids of all ages from every direction, some of them even your own. They'll tear through a tenpounder in no time and play seed-spitting games well until dark. Hose them all down when the melon is done. Hey, remember to save some for Momma!

Wheels

Once she got behind the wheel of that Chevy, Mom was never the same. Smack in the middle of humdrum, here was her paradise—with four-on-the-floor and chrome on the wheels. She wanted to tool down the highway and tear up the pavement and she could no longer stand standing still. Like a teenager first tasting freedom, Mom was always ready to ride. She'd bundle the two of us into the back, toss us a blanket, and take off for roads less traveled. We never knew where we were headed, and I don't think she cared. She drove for hours at a time, with all the windows open and a paisley scarf on her head. Sometimes we slept and awoke in magical places. We never got out except to pee, and I don't remember where she took us. It was never about arriving—it was always about Mom's wheels.

Wholeness

In a fragmented world, wholeness can be a challenge to sustain. You are pulled in so many directions; your energy scattered and bits and pieces flung hither and yon. Gather up the parts of yourself and bring them back into wholeness. Round out your edges and smooth yourself into a fullness that helps you respond instead of react. Balance your inner masculine and feminine: join your receptive yin and active yang into a glorious marriage of the whole. Nourish yourself and your family with whole foods and feel your physical health come 'round to wholeness. Embrace the wholeness of your spirituality and know that you are part of a grand and glorious whole. Do the math and understand: your whole is so much greater than the sum of your parts.

Wiggle

Give yourself room to wiggle at every turn. Shake
and shimmy your way behind the sofa to find the
missing markers and keep your fingers crossed
that they still have their caps on. Slither your arm
down and behind the back seat, wrap your fingers
around whatever they hit first, and give a good
yank. Get down and wiggle under the stall door
when your little trickster locks himself in at a
roadside rest stop. Wiggle across the grass to give
an up-close-and-personal look at the engineering
skills of ants. Use your wiggly wiles to get past
the doorkeeper who says, "No way, no how are
children allowed."

Wiggle your way through the climbing
tunnel at the playground, and pray that you
don't get stuck.

Let your kids wiggle their way out of
punishment once in a blue moon so they can
feel the power in wiggle.

Willingness

You'll find it works best if you're willing. Be
willing to try. Be willing to ask and be willing to
hear some new answers. Be willing to risk that
you might look foolish and you might end up
right back where you started. It never hurts to be
willing. Be willing to listen. Be willing to hear
your child out even if you're less than willing to
change your mind. On second thought, be willing
to change it. Willingness can go a long way if
you're willing to go there. Be willing to speak up
with a new voice. Be willing to surprise everybody. Before you say you'll do it, at least let them
know that you're willing. Are you willing to let go
of everything you hold dear? Willing to give all
you have and have faith you'll receive in return?
There's an infinite world when you find yourself
willing. There's great worth in willing, if only
you will.

Wind

Be aware of the wisdom that lives in the wind. How a gentle breeze can waft over you and soothe ruffled edges. How you can stand in the eye of a hurricane and find peace while around you everything is crashing and blowing to bits. Don't let a windy day keep you inside. Bundle everybody up and walk headlong into the wind. Feel yourself tested by a power you cannot control. Remember your place and be humble. Run with the wind with a child's hand in yours. Hear how he laughs and giggles at the touch of the wind, and never pushes up against the force of the wind. Keep the wind at your back and follow the path of least resistance, and your burden will always be lightened. Keep fighting and struggling and resisting the wind, and the wind will take the ground that you seek to attain.

Wisdom

One day you wake up and you've got wisdom. You might have gained it through age or inheritance or experience, but you know you've become rather wise. Wisdom is a deeper knowing than what you pick up in books or classes. What makes a woman wise is having enough discernment to sort through everything that's out there and take away what resonates inside. You can't go to a university for wisdom. There's no weekend workshop that will certify you wise. You gain wisdom through the college of hard knocks and through the school of life, and only after you've flunked the test at least as many times as you've passed it. A wise mother has seen enough and felt enough to understand why motherhood is the toughest job there ever was. Wisdom doesn't come fast and it doesn't come easy. Travel the path of a mother and in time you will surely turn wise.

Withdraw

You can search the shelves for supplements and tonics, but the only way to get over overwhelm is to withdraw. Get clear on your priorities and back off everything else. Politely decline your directorship for another year—and see who shows up with new energy and ideas. Attend fewer and fewer meetings, forget to sign up for anything, and take home no assignments. Withdraw from the school spotlight so someone else can step forward. Make an appearance now and then, but resist the pressure of perfect attendance. Some other mom can supervise. Somebody else can host. Surely there's another with a car who can drive. Ignore the idea that the association, the co-op, the hospital, the club, or the team can't make it without you. Create a space for someone who's ready to serve. The world has limped along for millennia without you. It can go a bit longer even if you withdraw.

Wonder

Wonder what it will feel like, how you will know.
Wonder about the pain, the joy. Wonder about the
magnificence of it all, the creation of new life, the
one born of two. Wonder if she'll have your hair,
his eyes, your granddaddy's gift for fixing anything
that ever broke. Your great-grandmother's knack
for seeing things just a split second before they
happen. Wonder about the life he'll lead. Whether
someday war will call out his name. Wonder how
it will be to watch them grow away from you, into
a world so different from your own. Wonder if
you'll feel like a real mother, or an impostor
playing dress-up. Wonder over and over again how
you could ever be a grandmother some day!
Imagine how you'll change as a woman, a partner,
a wife, a friend. Lose yourself in the miracle that
has made you a mother. Not the why, nor the how,
just the wonder.

Work

You may know what your job is, but do you know
your work? Have you listened to your inner
calling, to the sound of work crying out your
name? Have you claimed the work you were put
here to do, with the talents that you alone were
given? Your job may keep you in a windowless
office, while your work calls you to the great and
glorious outdoors. Your job may surround you
with policies and procedures, while your work
insists that you bust through old forms. Your
work will pay you a living while it also enlivens
your life. Your real work moves out from the core
of who you are, rather than just give you something to do. You may have a job that provides you
an income, yet ask yourself: am I doing my work?

Yes

Yes! You're having a baby. Yes! Everything is fine.
Yes! The papers are in order and the adoption is
final on Tuesday. The college said yes and you're
starting in September. The credit union said yes
and you're opening a store. The scout said yes and
your slugger is going to the minors. You asked
your sweetheart about Spain and there was yes in
his eyes. Yes, you accept the promotion to branch
manager. Yes, you'll relocate for the summer.
Renew your vows? Yes. Let your hair grow out?
Yes. Speak on behalf of concerned citizens at the
community meeting? Yes. Yes, you'll join the book
club. Yes, you'll make apricot preserves for the
fair. Will you take off a week and go cycling for
cancer research? They already know your answer.
Yes and yes and yes and yes. Asked the right question, you'll always say

Yes!

Yesterday

Sometimes the best thing you can say about yesterday is that it's over. Yesterday you drove the lawn mower into the petunias. Yesterday the bank called and your account is overdrawn. Yesterday nobody could find a single clean thing they wanted to wear, and everybody went off to school cranky. Was it only yesterday that you got the news about the twins? Was it that long ago that the sheriff called? Yesterday will go down in history as the day a certain someone used up her very last chance with the basketball coach. Not to mention with her mother. You served a new casserole that was loaded with broccoli and it wasn't much of a hit. Yesterday brought you one day closer to your final deadline but you didn't get much done. And on the topic of getting done: wasn't that some kind of yesterday?

Zip

Your life is loaded with zip. Zip up the boots and zip up the mittens. Zip up jackets and jeans and zipper-top bags. Unzip for potty and zip back up again. Oops! Careful with that zipper! Zip to the market. Zip to the drugstore. Zip to the bank on your way back home. Zip up the snowsuit, all six different zippers. Zip out the door, then zip right back in. Unzip for potty and zip back up again. Oops! Watch out with that zipper! The score's 32–zip and the team's lost its zing. Whip out some zippy new cheers. Zip through the checkout line in three minutes flat, while your little one zips up and down through the aisles. She's started unzipping, so zip up your wallet. Oops! Too late. The deed has been done. Your nickname should be Mom the Zipper.

About the Author

Rachel Snyder is the author of *365 Words of Well-Being for Women* (Contemporary Books, 1997) and *What There Is to Love About a Man* (Sourcebooks, 2000). Her inspirational and empowering words have appeared in *McCall's*, *American Baby*, and *The Women's Times*. She is the mother of two children and spends her time between Boulder, Colorado, and Torrey, Utah. Contact her at wordsofwellbeing.com.